DE-EXTINCTION

THE SCIENCE OF
BRINGING LOST SPECIES BACK TO LIFE

REBECCA E. HIRSCH

TWENTY-FIRST CENTURY BOOKS / MINNEAPOLIS

To Rick, for never-ending support

Twenty-First Century Books
A division of Lerner Publishing Group, Inc.
241 First Avenue North
Minneapolis, MN 55401 USA

For reading levels and more information, look up this title at www.lernerbooks.com.

Main body text set in Cheltenham ITC Std 11/15.
Typeface provided by International Typeface Corporation.

Library of Congress Cataloging-in-Publication Data

The Cataloging-in-Publication Data for *De-Extinction: The Science of Bringing Lost Species Back to Life* is on file at the Library of Congress.
ISBN 978-1-4677-9490-9 (lib. bdg.)
ISBN 978-1-5124-2848-3 (EB pdf)

Manufactured in the United States of America
1-38652-20544-9/14/2016

CONTENTS

CHAPTER ONE

THIS ILLUSTRATION OF A BUCARDO—A TYPE OF WILD GOAT—APPEARED IN AN 1898 BOOK CALLED *WILD OXEN, SHEEP, AND GOATS OF ALL LANDS, LIVING AND EXTINCT*. AT THE TIME OF THE BOOK'S PUBLICATION, BUCARDOS HAD NEARLY BEEN HUNTED TO EXTINCTION.

THE LAST BUCARDO

An air of excitement filled the room as the team readied for surgery. The date was July 30, 2003, and everyone was hoping for the best. With great care and skill, the team prepped the patient—a pregnant goat—and surgically delivered a 4.5-pound (2-kilogram) female kid. The newborn animal was a wild goat known as a bucardo.

The birth was a momentous achievement because, technically, the bucardo was extinct. The last of its kind had died three years earlier in the mountains of northern Spain. But there in the operating room, at a Spanish research facility, the bucardo had just flickered back into existence.

The newborn bucardo looked normal and had a normal heart rhythm, yet something was wrong. As Spanish wildlife veterinarian Alberto Fernández-Arias cradled the newborn in his arms, he could see that the animal was struggling to breathe. After only ten minutes, the baby bucardo died. Everyone in the room grew quiet. One person cried.

With that death, the bucardo once again passed into extinction.

DOLLY AND CELIA

For thousands of years, bucardos (*Capra pyrenaica pyrenaica*) roamed the Pyrenees. These mountains straddle the border between France and Spain. The animals had chestnut-colored coats of short, thick wool. Male bucardos sported long, ridged horns that curved backward in gentle arcs. The females, with smaller horns, looked similar to female deer.

Bucardos were well adapted to life in the mountains. They could clamber up steep cliffs and survive cold, snowy winters. During summer they lived high on the slopes, eating alpine plants. In winter they moved down to the valleys, where males and females mated. In spring females retreated to remote areas of the mountains to give birth.

Six hundred years ago, bucardos were common in the Pyrenees. Humans had little interaction with them. But their safety began changing when European game hunters discovered bucardos. Hunters shot the animals and mounted their heads on walls. Male heads, with their large, curving horns, were especially desired as trophies. In the nineteenth century, hunters from all over Europe traveled to the Pyrenees to seek this trophy animal, and the number of bucardos dwindled. Domestic livestock, brought into bucardo territory by farmers, may also have contributed to the decline. Some scientists theorize that farm animals competed with bucardos for food or passed on deadly diseases to them.

By 1900 fewer than one hundred bucardos were left. In the early twentieth century, the Spanish government created Ordesa National Park, which is off-limits to hunting. In the 1950s and 1960s, Spain created more wildlife refuges. Still the bucardo's numbers declined. By 1989 only about a dozen bucardos were left. In 1996 just three remained, and that year,

Dolly the sheep, who lived from 1996 to 2003, was the first mammal produced through cloning. De-extinctionists realized that the same techniques used to create Dolly could be used to revive extinct species.

two of them died natural deaths. Scientists realized the animal could not be saved from its slide into extinction. "That was the hardest year," said Fernández-Arias.

Also in 1996, Scottish scientists achieved a historic first, cloning a sheep that they named Dolly. A cloned animal is a living animal created not by sexual reproduction but by manipulating reproductive cells in a laboratory. Clones differ from other animals in the way they acquire their genes (the material inside cells that controls how an organism grows, behaves, and reproduces).

INSIDE THE GENOME

Deoxyribonucleic acid (DNA) directs the growth and development of all living things. DNA molecules are coiled up inside chromosomes, threadlike structures inside cells.

A DNA molecule is shaped like a twisted rope ladder. Chemical compounds called nucleotides make up the strands of the ladder. Parts of those compounds, called bases, make up the rungs of the ladder. These bases are adenine, thymine, guanine, and cytosine, designated by the letters: A, T, G, and C. The sequence, or arrangement, of the bases in DNA determines an organism's traits. Specific segments of DNA are called genes.

The complete set of DNA in an organism is known as its genome. The genome resides in the nucleus of each cell, where it is packaged into chromosomes. The genome contains all the information needed to build and maintain a particular organism. Genomes are enormous and very complex. The human genome, for example, is made of roughly three billion base pairs and contains about thirty thousand genes spread over twenty-three pairs of chromosomes.

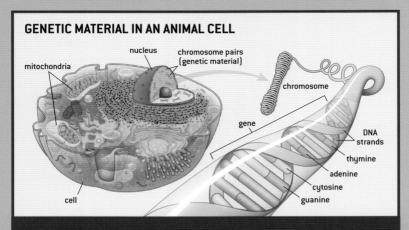

GENETIC MATERIAL IN AN ANIMAL CELL

nucleus

chromosome pairs (genetic material)

mitochondria

chromosome

gene

DNA strands

thymine

adenine

cytosine

guanine

cell

DNA, which is packed into chromosomes inside cell nuclei, holds instructions for how living things behave, grow, and reproduce. Specific segments of DNA are called genes. Geneticists can manipulate genes in the laboratory to change an organism's traits.

Organisms produced via sexual reproduction get half their genes from one parent and half from the other. Clones, on the other hand, have the exact same genes as only one parent. The birth of Dolly the sheep, the first mammal produced by cloning, was a scientific leap that made news around the world. That achievement brought hope that the bucardo could also be cloned to save it from extinction.

In April 1999, Fernández-Arias led a team into the mountains to find the last bucardo, a female nicknamed Celia. The scientists took samples of Celia's blood and feces, scraped some skin from her ear for genetic testing, and snapped a collar on her to track her movements via radio. Then they released her back into the wild.

On January 6, 2000, Celia's radio collar gave a long, sustained beep. That signal meant that Celia was no longer moving—she had died. When researchers found her, they saw that her skull had been crushed by a fallen tree. With Celia's death, the bucardo had passed into extinction.

A species or subspecies (a subdivision of a species) becomes extinct when all of its kind have died. But in the bucardo's case, although Celia had died, some of her cells—extracted from her blood and skin in 1999—still lived. Fernández-Arias and his team had frozen the cells in liquid nitrogen at a temperature of –321°F (–196°C). Scientists wondered, What if they could use the cells to clone Celia and bring the bucardo back to life? Could they reverse extinction?

CLONING CELIA

After Celia's death, a team led by José Folch, one of the scientists who had helped collar Celia, began trying to clone her in a laboratory in Spain. Using the same technology that the Scottish scientists had used to clone Dolly the sheep, the Spanish team carried out somatic cell nuclear transfer, also called nuclear transfer. A somatic cell is any cell in the body other than a sperm or egg cell. Sperm and eggs are germ cells, or reproductive cells. During sexual reproduction, a sperm cell fuses with an egg cell, in a process called fertilization. Once an egg is fertilized, it divides and becomes an embryo, an unborn or unhatched offspring.

Cloning produces offspring differently. To clone Celia, researchers took an egg cell from a domestic goat and removed its nucleus, the compartment inside a cell that holds the deoxyribonucleic acid (DNA), the genetic material that directs the growth and development of all living things. The team then fused one of Celia's somatic cells with the empty egg cell using a pulse of electricity. Then they bathed the fused cell in chemicals to stimulate cell division. The goat egg cell, which then contained the nucleus of Celia's somatic cell, began behaving like a fertilized egg. The egg had come from the goat, but all the egg's DNA came from Celia.

Because success rates for cloning are low, Folch's team used goat egg cells and Celia's somatic cells to make more than 150 eggs. They implanted the eggs into the wombs of surrogate mothers. The mothers were either domestic goats or hybrid animals—the offspring of two different species. In this case, they were the offspring of domestic goats and Spanish ibexes, a type of wild European goat. The scientists implanted 154 eggs in forty-four females. Of this group, seven females became pregnant. Of those seven pregnancies, six ended in miscarriage. Just one surrogate animal carried her pregnancy to term. That's the animal that gave birth to the female bucardo in July 2003. The baby bucardo was a clone

To clone Celia, scientists fused one of her somatic cells with an egg cell from a domestic goat. They implanted the resulting embryo into a surrogate mother. The cloned bucardo was born alive but soon died.

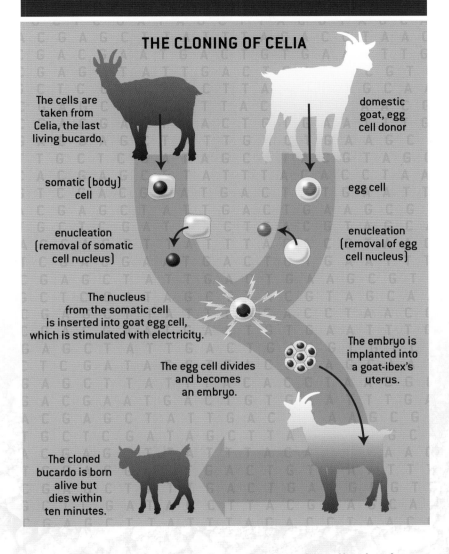

THE CLONING OF CELIA

The cells are taken from Celia, the last living bucardo.

domestic goat, egg cell donor

somatic (body) cell

egg cell

enucleation (removal of somatic cell nucleus)

enucleation (removal of egg cell nucleus)

The nucleus from the somatic cell is inserted into goat egg cell, which is stimulated with electricity.

The egg cell divides and becomes an embryo.

The embryo is implanted into a goat-ibex's uterus.

The cloned bucardo is born alive but dies within ten minutes.

of (genetically identical to) Celia. But the clone lived only ten minutes. An autopsy later revealed that one of her lungs was deformed. Birth defects and early death are common problems with cloned animals.

Despite the failure, disappointment, and sadness, the scientists had achieved their ambitious goal. They had brought an extinct animal back to life for the first time in history.

A STRUGGLE FOR SURVIVAL

Extinction is a natural part of life on Earth. Scientists tell us that more than 99 percent of all living things that have ever existed have gone extinct. Extinction goes hand in hand with evolution, the process by which new species develop.

To understand evolution, consider a population of seed-eating sparrows on a remote island. Although all the sparrows have inherited traits from their parents, each individual sparrow is unique. This variation arises from naturally occurring differences in genes.

Every year, the adult sparrows produce offspring, and many of them die before becoming adults. Some die because they can't find enough food. Predators such as hawks eat other young sparrows. But some offspring survive to adulthood because of favorable traits unique to them. For instance, maybe some sparrows have bigger beaks than others and can therefore crack open larger seeds, giving them access to food that is unavailable to sparrows with smaller beaks. Maybe some sparrows are better camouflaged, with feather colors that blend well into their surroundings, so hawks don't see them. The sparrows with larger beaks and better camouflage are more likely to survive and reproduce.

The survival of animals or plants with favorable traits is called natural selection. In natural selection, organisms that are best adapted to their environment are the ones most likely to survive and have offspring. They pass on their favorable traits to their offspring, which pass the traits to their offspring, and so on.

WHAT'S IN A NAME—OR TWO OR THREE?

All plants and animals have common names, such as the African clawed frog or the Yangtze River dolphin. Biologists also use a scientific naming system created by Swedish scientist Carolus Linnaeus in the mid-eighteenth century. The system uses Latin-based terms to identify each plant or animal's genus (a group of closely related animals) and species (specific kind within that group). For example, the scientific name for gray wolves is *Canis lupis*. *Canis* is the genus name, and *lupis* is the species name.

Genus and species are the most precise classifications for living things. But these categories fall under a larger naming umbrella consisting of eight levels: domain, kingdom, phylum, class, order, family, genus, and species. You can see the hierarchy by looking at gray wolves. They belong to the domain Eukarya—a group that includes all plants, animals, and fungi, as well as single-celled organisms called protists. Within that category, gray wolves belong to the kingdom Animalia (the animal kingdom), the phylum Chordata (animals with backbones), the class Mammalia (mammals, animals that have hair or fur and nurse their young), the order Carnivora (mammals with sharp teeth and claws, including bears, cats, and doglike animals), the family Canidae (doglike mammals), and the genus *Canis* (specific kinds of doglike mammals). The species name *Canis lupus* is the specific designation for the gray wolf. Each kind of living thing has its own species name, and members of the same species can mate with one another.

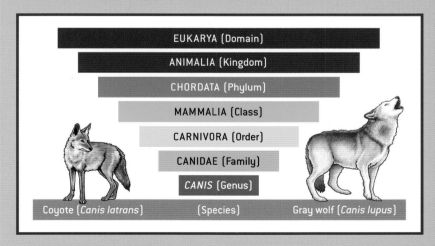

EUKARYA (Domain)

ANIMALIA (Kingdom)

CHORDATA (Phylum)

MAMMALIA (Class)

CARNIVORA (Order)

CANIDAE (Family)

CANIS (Genus)

Coyote (*Canis latrans*)   (Species)   Gray wolf (*Canis lupus*)

Over time, organisms with favorable traits become more common in the population. Over many generations, natural selection can even create new species. British naturalist Charles Darwin first described natural selection in his 1859 book *On the Origin of Species*.

Natural selection can also lead to extinction. Let's also imagine that a new group of seed-eating birds moves to the island, perhaps blown there in a storm. The new birds compete for food with the local sparrows. Whichever species is better suited for the island environment will survive. The other species might go extinct.

MASS EXTINCTIONS

For most of the history of life on Earth, the rate of extinction was low and steady. This slow drip-drip-drip of extinctions is known as background extinction. But five times in Earth's history, the extinction rate jumped dramatically. During events known as mass extinctions, huge numbers of living things died out quickly.

Scientists aren't sure exactly what caused the mass extinctions, but they probably involved chains of events. In some cases, natural climate shifts likely killed off great numbers of species. In other cases, massive volcanic eruptions or an asteroid striking Earth set off a deadly chain reaction by throwing huge amounts of dust and debris into the atmosphere. This material would have darkened the sky for months on end, preventing sunlight from reaching the ground. It would have killed off many plants and the animals that relied on them for food. The initial eruption or asteroid impact might also have released heat-trapping gases into the atmosphere. The gases would have warmed the air and

Since life on Earth began more than 3.5 billion years ago, the planet has experienced five mass extinctions. They took place about 450 million years ago, 359 million years ago, 250 million years ago, 200 million years ago, and 65 million years ago. In modern times, because of human activities, plant and animal species are going extinct extremely rapidly. Many scientists say that Earth is in the midst of a sixth extinction.

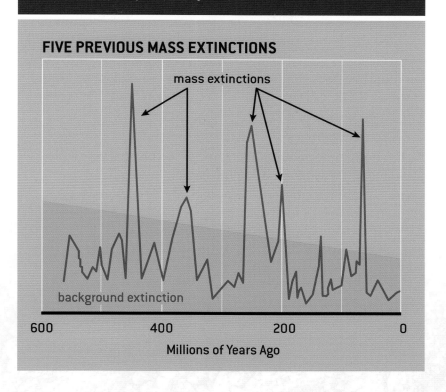

FIVE PREVIOUS MASS EXTINCTIONS

mass extinctions

background extinction

600   400   200   0

Millions of Years Ago

dramatically changed the temperature and chemistry of the oceans. Those changes would have caused even more species to go extinct.

The first mass extinction identified by scientists occurred about 450 million years ago, when most organisms still lived in Earth's oceans. The deadliest was the third extinction, about 250 million years ago, when more than 90 percent of all living things vanished over a span of about 60,000 years. The fifth extinction, possibly caused by an asteroid strike, happened 65 million years ago. This is when most dinosaurs died out. The fifth extinction ushered in our own geologic era, the Cenozoic. This era is also called the Age of Mammals because after the demise of the dinosaurs, which were reptiles, mammals became the dominant category of land animals. The Cenozoic is also when our own species, *Homo sapiens*, appeared, about two hundred thousand years ago on the grasslands of Africa.

THE SIXTH EXTINCTION

As the human population has grown to almost seven billion people and become more technologically advanced, we've come to dominate life on the planet. We've also driven up extinction rates, in four main ways.

First, we kill. On purpose. We hunt and fish animals for food and for pleasure, and we collect or chop down plants for food and to burn as fuel—but to excess. Direct killing

Deforestation hurts animal species in several ways. For one thing, it destroys habitat, the natural homes where animals normally live, find food, and find mating partners. Deforestation also contributes to climate change because trees absorb carbon dioxide from the air. With fewer trees, carbon dioxide levels climb even higher, trapping more heat near Earth and leading to more extreme weather.

has wiped out a long list of species, including the bucardo, a bird called the dodo (*Raphus cucullatus*), and the passenger pigeon (*Ectopistes migratorius*), which was once the most numerous bird on the planet.

Second, we destroy habitat, or the natural homes of plants and animals, to build cities, roads, and suburbs. We bulldoze wetlands and forests for farming and housing developments. We dig up the ground in enormous mining operations to extract coal, copper, and other valuable substances. Through these activities, we wipe out the natural homes of living things, the spaces plants and animals need to survive. We also carve up habitat into ragged patches. For example, workers might build a major highway through wild animal habitat, dividing the habitat into two or more sections. The highway creates a barrier, and animals risk their lives when they cross it through traffic to get to the other part of their habitat. When habitats are too small or are carved up, animals have trouble finding enough food to survive. They also have more difficulty finding other animals of the same species with which to breed. This carving of the landscape into small pieces is called habitat fragmentation.

Third, we move species where they don't belong. When we move ourselves and our goods around the world, we sometimes bring along dangerous hitchhikers: plants and animals that are not native to the new regions. Without local predators to check their numbers, the nonnative species can do great harm to ecosystems (complex communities of living things and their environment). The newcomers can spread diseases to local animals, which have no resistance to the new illnesses. For example, before the 1970s, medical supply companies shipped African clawed frogs (*Xenopus laevis*) from their central and southern African homes to cities around the world, where scientists and researchers used them in lab studies and pregnancy tests. (In the pregnancy tests, medical workers injected a woman's urine into a female frog. If the woman was pregnant, a hormone in her urine caused the frog to lay eggs. Scientists have since developed pregnancy tests that do not involve frogs.) African clawed frogs carry the chytrid fungus (*Batrachochytrium dendrobatidis*) but don't get sick from it themselves. However, the chytrid fungus can kill other amphibians (animals such as frogs, toads, and salamanders that spend part of their lives in water and part on land). When individual frogs escaped from laboratories or were released into the wild, they spread the fungus into frog habitats around the world. Scientists say that the chytrid fungus has probably caused the extinction of more than one hundred different amphibian species worldwide.

Fourth, we pollute. One victim of pollution was the Yangtze River dolphin (*Lipotes vexillifer*), which was last spotted in the wild in 2004. It likely went extinct in part because its home, the Yangtze River in China, became heavily polluted with chemicals from nearby farms and factories. One of the most dangerous forms of pollution in the modern world is carbon dioxide, a heat-trapping gas that is released into the atmosphere when people burn fossil fuels (coal, oil, and natural gas). We've poured so much carbon dioxide into the atmosphere from our motor vehicles and manufacturing plants that we are changing the global climate. Climate change has led to higher temperatures and more weather extremes, including droughts and floods. The changes in climate are happening so fast that species worldwide are struggling to adapt and many are dying. "As a human species, we have been amazingly efficient at making things extinct," says conservation biologist Kate Jones of University College London.

Water pollution in China killed off the Yangtze River dolphin. The last time anyone spotted a dolphin in the river was in 2004.

The Switzerland-based International Union for Conservation of Nature (IUCN) keeps track of extinction risks for species across the planet. As of 2016, the IUCN reports that 13 percent of birds, 26 percent of mammals, and 42 percent of amphibians are threatened with extinction. Other scientists say that the rates of modern extinction are one hundred to one thousand times greater than normal background extinction. For this reason, many scientists say that Earth is in the midst of a sixth extinction, the worst since the dinosaurs disappeared sixty-five million years ago. If current trends continue, some experts predict that by the year 2100, nearly half of all species currently living on Earth could be gone forever. That would make the sixth extinction the fastest in Earth's history.

THE WEB OF LIFE

Life on Earth depends on biodiversity, or having many kinds of organisms in an ecosystem. Biodiversity is important because plants and animals in an environment rely on one another for survival. When an animal goes extinct or when an ecosystem loses a key species, the loss can harm other species in that ecosystem as well. One well-studied example is the loss of gray wolves *(Canis lupus)* from Yellowstone National Park in Wyoming, Idaho, and Montana in the 1930s. The wolves disappeared from the park (and much of the western United States) after years of killing by hunters, ranchers, and farmers. The loss of this important predator rippled through the ecosystem. Without wolves to prey on them, the park's elk population grew. Herds of elk fed heavily on willow shrubs along stream banks, stripping the vegetation to the ground. Willows serve as food and dam-building material for beavers, and with fewer willow shrubs, the park's beaver population dwindled. Without beavers, beaver ponds disappeared, along with many of the plants and animals that depended on the ponds for food and habitat. So the loss of one key species dramatically changed the park's ecosystem.

Wildlife workers reintroduced wolves to the park starting in the mid-1990s, with mixed results. In some parts of the park, the ecosystem began to recover. Willows grew back in lush stands, and as the willows came back, so did the beavers. But in other areas, willows still have not recovered and beavers have not returned. Some researchers say that in those areas, the damage from the wolves' long absence may be irreversible. It is a sobering sign of the permanent harm caused when a member of an ecosystem goes missing, even if that member later returns.

The extinction of species can also impact human life. Consider animal pollinators—the birds, bats, and insects that, while searching for nectar and pollen inside flowers, carry pollen from flower to flower. Pollination enables flowering plants to bear fruit and produce seeds that will grow into new plants. Nearly 90 percent of the world's flowering plants depend on animal pollinators for reproduction. In turn, many animals, including humans, rely on these plants for food. One out of every three bites of food for humans would not exist without animal pollinators. If Earth were less biodiverse, with fewer pollinators, people would lose valuable foods, such as almonds, apples, peaches, cherries, melons, coffee, and chocolate. Dairy products would also be at risk, as dairy cows eat alfalfa, another crop pollinated by animals. A wealth of scientific studies shows that wild pollinators are declining in North America and Europe. Declines have been reported in South America, Africa, Asia, and Oceania too, although pollinators aren't as well studied in those parts of the world. The reasons for the declines are complex, but scientists believe pollinators may be succumbing to a lethal mix of pesticides (insect-killing chemicals) and other pollutants, habitat loss, invasive species, and climate change. One thing that is clear is that the loss of pollinators puts the human food supply at risk.

After humans killed off the wolves in Yellowstone National Park in the 1930s, their disappearance affected elks, willow trees, beavers, and other plant and animal species. Wolves were reintroduced to the park in the 1990s.

REVERSING EXTINCTION

In the current extinction crisis, many thousands of species are at risk of disappearing forever. Once they are gone, we cannot bring them back. Extinction is essentially a one-way street. Or is it? What if we could bring back lost species? By bringing them back, in a process called de-extinction, maybe we could restore lost ecosystems, providing healthy habitat for existing and revived species. Can we do this? *Should* we?

The answers are murky. Many people—both scientists and nonscientists—are opposed to de-extinction. Some biologists say that de-extinction is a bad idea, one that could divert money and attention from efforts to save species that are endangered but not yet extinct. Some critics raise moral and ethical concerns, saying that de-extinction amounts to scientists "playing God" with nature.

Despite these objections, a group of people who support de-extinction—prominent scientists and their allies—are pressing forward with the idea that extinction need not be final. Using frozen cells, ancient DNA, and genetic engineering (altering the genes of living things), they are hard at work trying to reverse extinction and return some lost species safely to the wild.

Some de-extinctionists are focusing on recently extinct animals, such as the passenger pigeon, a bird that has been extinct for only about one hundred years. Others are gazing more deeply into the prehistoric past, at creatures such as the woolly mammoth (*Mammuthus primigenius*), an animal that has been extinct for thousands of years. Some scientists are trying to create exact replicas of extinct animals. Others are editing, or altering, the DNA of living animals to make it more closely resemble the DNA of extinct species.

Some biologists argue that the best use of de-extinction technology isn't to bring back extinct animals. They say that instead, the techniques are most promising for helping endangered animals and keeping them from sliding into extinction in the first place. They want to use de-extinction technology to boost numbers of endangered animals and to rebuild healthy animal populations that can survive in the wild.

In the emerging field of de-extinction, the 2003 revival of Celia was a watershed moment. That event marked the first time that scientists had revived, however briefly, an extinct animal. It was the world's first de-extinction.

Scientists say that it almost certainly will not be the last.

CHAPTER TWO

DURING THE LAST ICE AGE, WHICH ENDED ABOUT 11,500 YEARS AGO, WOOLLY MAMMOTHS MADE THEIR HOMES ACROSS EUROPE, ASIA, AND NORTH AMERICA. THE SPECIES WENT EXTINCT AT THE END OF THE ICE AGE. THIS ILLUSTRATION OF ICE AGE NORTHERN SPAIN SHOWS SEVERAL MAMMOTHS *(CENTER)*, ALONG WITH A WOOLLY RHINOCEROS *(RIGHT)* AND OTHER ICE AGE ANIMALS.

RESURRECTING
THE MAMMOTH

A herd of mammoths stops beside a raging river. A month-old calf seeks safety under her mother's enormous, furry body. Spring has come to the grassy steppe (grassland), and the herd is marching north toward summer pastures. An icy wind howls across the thawing grassland. The river runs high with melted snow.

The mother turns her attention away, and the calf wanders out from under her and toward the river. But the riverbank is muddy, and the calf loses her footing. She slides halfway down the slope before her mother spots her. The mother trumpets in alarm, and the rest of the herd rushes over. Several adults try to wrap their trunks around the calf, but she slides farther down the slippery slope, out of reach. As the calf struggles, her body sinks into the soft muck. Mud fills her mouth, her throat, and her lungs. The calf struggles more but only sinks deeper. Soon she disappears into the soft ground. The herd lingers, but the baby mammoth does not reappear. Finally, the herd turns and continues its march northward. That scene—or something like it—took place forty-two thousand years ago.

A REMARKABLE FIND

On a spring day in 2007, a reindeer herder named Yuri Khudi stood with three of his sons on the banks of the Yuribey River in northern Russia. They had found an animal corpse sticking out of the snow. It was a baby mammoth, almost perfectly preserved. Khudi left the carcass and traveled 150 miles (241 kilometers) to the nearest village, where he and a friend alerted the director of the local museum to their discovery.

Officials named the baby mammoth Lyuba, in honor of Khudi's wife. Khudi's find was possibly the most well-preserved carcass of a woolly mammoth ever discovered.

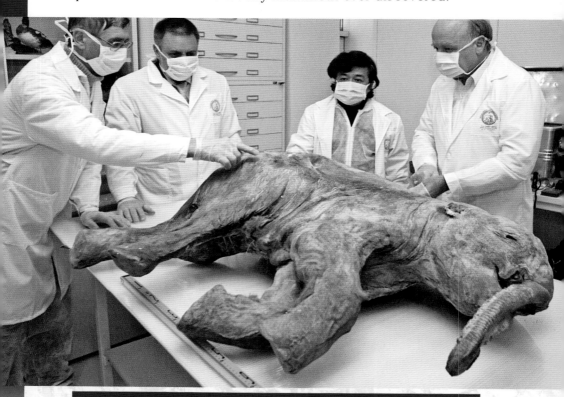

An international team of scientists examines the body of Lyuba, a baby woolly mammoth discovered preserved in the frozen ground of northern Russia in 2007.

The animal's skin was intact, and although most of the hair was missing, here and there a few tufts remained. Of the entire body, only the tail was gone. Lyuba's stomach even contained traces of her mother's milk.

Lyuba was one month old when she died forty-two thousand years ago. No one knows precisely how she died, although her body gave some clues. During an autopsy, researchers discovered fine mud in her mouth, throat, and lungs. This suggests that she choked to death while sinking into the mud.

Scientists have looked to Lyuba and other mammoth specimens with great hope. Could such a well-preserved specimen hold within it a remarkable prize, something that has long eluded science? Could it contain intact cells—whole cells with no breaks in the cell membrane and containing whole, undecayed chromosomes—that could be used to clone a woolly mammoth?

WHEN MAMMOTHS WALKED THE EARTH

The earliest mammoths lived millions of years ago in tropical Africa, alongside a related group of animals, the ancestors of modern elephants. Mammoths later spread into Europe and Asia. From Asia they crossed into North America over a land bridge that once connected the northeastern tip of Asia to the northwestern tip of North America. Herds of mammoths traveled eastward across this bridge at two different times, about one and a half million years ago and again about one hundred thousand years ago. The bridge has since been covered by seawater.

Over thousands and thousands of years, mammoths in different places evolved into distinct species. The woolly mammoth is the most famous and best understood because of millions of frozen carcasses preserved in the permafrost (permanently frozen soil) in Arctic regions, where the animals were once plentiful. Full-grown woolly mammoths stood 9 to 11 feet (2.7 to 3.3 meters) tall at the shoulder and weighed 8,000 to 12,000 pounds (3,630 to 5,440 kg), about the size of modern African elephants. They had small ears; long, twisting tusks; thick layers of fat; and long, shaggy coats. Woolly mammoths lived in a nutrient-rich, dry grassland known as the mammoth steppe. It once extended across northern Europe, northern Asia, and northern North America.

A less shaggy mammoth, the Columbian mammoth, lived farther south, across much of the lands that became the United States and Mexico. Columbian mammoths were bigger than their woolly cousins. They stood up to 14 feet (4.3 m) tall at the shoulder and weighed as much as 22,000 pounds (9,980 kg), with tusks measuring 16 feet (4.9 m) or longer.

Besides the two species of mainland mammoths, populations of dwarf mammoths inhabited several islands around the world: Wrangel Island off the northeastern coast of Russia, the Channel Islands near California, and Sardinia in

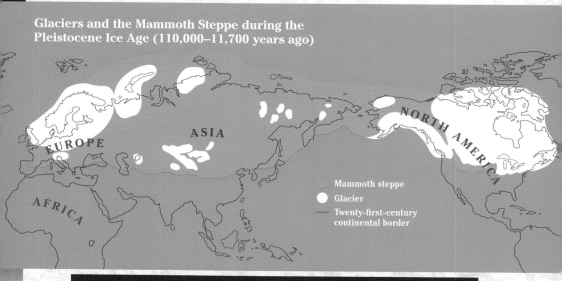

Glaciers and the Mammoth Steppe during the Pleistocene Ice Age (110,000–11,700 years ago)

EUROPE

ASIA

AFRICA

NORTH AMERICA

○ Mammoth steppe
● Glacier
— Twenty-first-century continental border

During the last ice age, a grassland called the mammoth steppe covered much of Europe, North America, and Asia. It was home to woolly mammoths, woolly rhinoceroses, bison, horses, reindeer, yaks, and other grazing animals.

MAMMOTH EVOLUTION

Woolly mammoths evolved from a species of ancient elephants. Natural selection might have driven this evolution. Scientists don't know exactly what happened, but they think that perhaps some ancient elephants had more fur than others. The elephants with thick fur would have survived in a cold environment better than those with less fur. These elephants would have lived longer and produced more offspring, which also would have had thick fur. Over time, as natural selection continued, the entire population of elephants would have had thick fur coats. Along with other changes, this might have resulted in the emergence of an entirely new elephant species: woolly mammoths.

What caused mammoths living on islands to become smaller than mainland mammoths? Natural selection explains that too. Animals living on islands often have a limited food supply. If they don't swim or fly, they can't leave the island to find more food elsewhere during food shortages. Smaller animals need less food and thus are more likely than large animals to survive food shortages. So the small mammoths on islands may have been more likely to survive and have offspring, which also would have been small. The offspring pass on this trait to their offspring as well. This would have led to the eventual creation of a population of dwarf mammoths.

the Mediterranean Sea. The dwarf mammoths, some not much taller than a goat, were the descendants of full-sized, mainland mammoths that had swum to the islands and settled there.

For thousands of years, the different species of mammoths lived in North America, Europe, and Asia. And then, at about the same time, across every continent and on every island, they all went extinct. The mainland mammoths disappeared about 11,500 years ago. The dwarf mammoths hung on longer. The last surviving dwarf mammoths, on Wrangel Island, vanished about 3,500 years ago.

In all cases, the cause of extinction is unknown. Some scientists blame climate change. Beginning about 14,700 years ago, Earth's climate shifted, and the world became warmer and wetter. Mammoths failed to adapt to the new conditions, some say. Other researchers think ancient humans hunted mammoths to extinction. But most researchers suspect that mammoths were done in by both climate change and hunting.

CLUES FROM THE PAST

Mammoths may have disappeared from the world, but their remains have not. Researchers have pulled many woolly mammoth carcasses from the frozen soil.

Modern climate change is bringing even more mammoth remains to the surface. Rising temperatures are melting and eroding the permafrost in Siberia (a province in north central Russia) and other cold places where woolly mammoths once roamed. As the ground softens, more and more carcasses are exposed. Some, such as Lyuba, are remarkably well preserved.

Scientists know that woolly mammoths behaved a lot like modern elephants. Similar to African elephants, woolly mammoths were grazers, eating grasses rather than the leaves of trees and shrubs. Scientists have determined this by looking at evidence of grasses in fossilized mammoth dung (dung that over thousands of years has turned to stone) and also by examining the stomach contents of preserved mammoths. Scientists know that mammoths, like modern elephants, lived in large family groups, since fossilized mammoth tracks show adults and young mammoths walking side by side. Scientists also know that as with elephants, the family groups consisted mostly of females. Males were kicked out of the herds at adolescence, behavior that is revealed in the preserved tusks of males.

Tusks grow in rings, with new ivory developing in the center of the tusk and building up in layers over time, with a distinct ring added each year. As with tree rings, the number of tusk rings reveals a mammoth's age, and the thickness of the rings is a record of how much nutrition the animal was getting at different points in its lifetime. "In teenage males, the growth rings in the tusks become suddenly narrow," explains Jacquelyn Gill, an ecologist at the University of Maine, "indicating that the male suddenly had to fend for itself." Gill calls this shift the mammoth equivalent of "going from your parents' home-cooked meals to the macaroni and cheese and ramen [noodle] diets of your first apartment." Scientists know that mammoth males, like elephant males, fought each other in competition over mates. This competition is revealed by broken tusks and, in one case, a pair of male skeletons locked together in battle.

The wealth of remains has led not only to clues about mammoths' past but to ideas about their future. What if woolly mammoths could be revived? If a source of intact mammoth cells was found, could the species be brought back to life through cloning?

RECIPE FOR RESURRECTION

Mammoths might be resurrected in several different ways. If scientists located an intact cell, containing intact chromosomes, within frozen mammoth hair, bones, or other tissue, they could coax the cell to divide, making a supply of new mammoth cells. They then could take an egg cell from a female Asian elephant (the woolly mammoth's closest living relative), remove its nucleus, and insert the nucleus from a mammoth cell in its place. Scientists could then stimulate the egg to start dividing and implant the resulting embryo into a female elephant.

HOW OLD IS THAT BONE?

Our knowledge of extinct species draws on fossil specimens, some dating back millions of years. A fossil is the preserved remains or traces of a living thing. Fossils take different forms. Some are rocks. They form when mineral-rich water percolates into dead plant or animal tissue, and the minerals gradually replace the tissue. Other fossils are insects preserved in amber, the hardened sap of ancient trees. Some fossils, such as some ancient bones and teeth, are preserved as organic matter, the same substance they had when the animal was alive.

When paleontologists (scientists who study life from past geological eras) determine the age of fossils, they can then match the fossils to the dates of known changes in the environment. They can answer such questions as, "Did this kind of animal become extinct during a time of climate change?" or "Did many other animals go extinct at the same time as this one?" Finding correlations can help scientists understand the causes of extinction.

To date fossils, scientists might compare them to other fossils whose age has already been established or to the rock layers in which they are found, a method known as relative dating. Sedimentary rocks— rocks formed from layers of built-up sediment— are common on Earth. In these rocks, higher layers are typically younger (more recent) than deeper layers. So a fossil preserved in a higher layer will be younger than another fossil preserved deeper in the rock.

Some of the fossils in this picture are ancient sea animals that lived on Earth during the Mississippian period, between about 318 and 359 million years ago. Their remains long ago turned into stone.

A more precise method is called carbon 14 dating. While they are living, plants and animals take in a radioactive substance called carbon 14. Plants absorb it from the air, and animals get it from the plants they eat. After death, organisms no longer take in carbon 14. Over time, the carbon 14 remaining in their tissues decays and turns into nitrogen. Because of this decay, older fossils have less carbon 14 than younger fossils. The decay happens at a constant, known rate, so paleontologists can measure the amount of carbon 14 in a fossil and estimate its age. Carbon dating is useful only for fossils that are made of organic matter (not those that have turned into rock) and only for those younger than about fifty thousand years. Older fossils contain too little carbon 14 to make accurate measurements.

To date fossils older than forty thousand years, paleontologists turn to substances in tissues that have slower rates of decay. For example, they can measure uranium in tissue to date fossils that are several hundred thousand years old, and they can measure a form of potassium to date fossils that are millions of years old.

If the pregnancy were successful, in twenty-two months, the female elephant would give birth to a baby mammoth. This is similar to the cloning technique that scientists used to revive the bucardo.

With a newer technique, scientists could create mammoth embryos more directly. Young embryos are made of stem cells, cells that have the ability to turn into many different cell types. As an embryo grows, the stem cells change in structure and function and turn into specific somatic cells, such as muscle or immune cells. This change occurs when some genes switch on in the somatic cells while others switch off. In 2006 scientists Kazutoshi Takahashi and Shinya Yamanaka at Kyoto University in Japan discovered that they could reverse the process and turn somatic cells back into immature stem cells. They accomplished this reversal with mouse cells using transcription factors. These are the proteins that bind to DNA and turn on and off groups of genes. Yamanaka shared the 2012 Nobel Prize in Physiology or Medicine with British biologist John Gurdon for this discovery.

Scientists could theoretically use the ability to return somatic cells to an embryonic state to clone a woolly mammoth. If researchers could find intact woolly mammoth somatic cells, such as muscle cells, they could use transcription factors to turn the somatic cells into stem cells. They could then stimulate the cells to grow into embryos, which could be implanted into the wombs of female elephants. If pregnancies (achieved by either cloning technique) resulted in healthy baby mammoths, eventually male and female mammoths could be bred to produce more mammoth offspring.

A third way to revive the species is through artificial insemination. In this procedure, sperm from a male animal

Nigel Larkin, a conservator with a British museum, holds a mammoth molar taken from a dig in Swaffham, Great Britain. Mammoth remains might hold intact DNA that can be used in de-extinction efforts.

are inserted into the uterus of a female. Doctors frequently use this method to help women become pregnant. To make artificial insemination work in mammoths, scientists would have to find intact mammoth sperm cells. Scientists would use the ancient sperm to impregnate a female elephant, resulting in a hybrid mammoth–elephant offspring. Additional hybrids could be produced with more mammoth sperm, and the resulting animals could be mated with one another. Over several generations, the offspring of such mating would be more and more mammoth-like.

BROKEN CELLS AND DAMAGED DNA

Researchers from South Korea and Russia have teamed up to look for intact cells within mammoth remains in the Siberian permafrost. They have searched the tundra (treeless lands covered with ice and snow for most of the year) for remains. They have examined mammoth bone marrow, hair, skin, and fat. Japanese scientists have been searching for mammoth sperm to use for artificial insemination. So far no one has found anything useful. They have found broken cells but no intact cells. No sperm. No intact chromosomes.

Other scientists doubt that intact mammoth cells, sperm, or chromosomes will ever be found. That's because mammoth carcasses undergo repeated cycles of thawing and freezing as the seasons change year after year. These cycles cause cells to break open. Microorganisms such as bacteria settle in and cause the cells and their DNA to decay further. Eske Willerslev, a geneticist at the University of Copenhagen in Denmark, said that researchers have contacted him requesting mammoth tissue for cloning experiments. "I don't think they will find anything they can use," he remarks.

What about well-preserved mammoths like Lyuba? Appearances can be deceiving. Although Lyuba's body looks perfectly preserved, her cells and DNA are not. Lyuba's remains give off a strong, sour odor. It is the smell of lactic acid, produced by bacteria. Although the acid has kept the carcass from rotting, it has also destroyed Lyuba's cells and DNA.

Beth Shapiro, a paleogeneticist (a scientist who studies the past using DNA from fossils) at the University of California–Santa Cruz is the author of *How to Clone a Mammoth: The Science of De-extinction*. She writes, "Mammoth cloning is not going to happen. No intact genomes will have survived the 3,700 years since the last mammoths walked on Wrangel Island. No mammoth chromosomes will be found. . . . It doesn't matter how many trips are made to deepest Siberia."

A few scientists continue searching for intact mammoth cells. But other scientists say that cloning is not the only way to revive the mammoth.

A paleontologist examines fossils at a "dinosaur graveyard"—a deposit containing thousands of bones—in eastern Spain. Could we use DNA from the bones to clone new dinosaurs? The answer is no. The DNA decayed tens of millions of years ago.

WHY WE'LL NEVER CLONE DINOSAURS

The 1993 movie *Jurassic Park* and its many sequels, which feature a theme park filled with cloned dinosaurs, left many moviegoers with the impression that cloning dinosaurs from ancient dinosaur DNA is possible. Whether or not you think it's wise to bring back *Tyrannosaurus rex*, scientists say it is not possible. Dinosaur DNA is simply too old.

A half-life is the amount of time it takes for half of a substance to disintegrate through natural processes. The half-life of DNA is the time it takes for half of the nucleotide bonds (chemical connections in a strand of DNA) in a given amount of DNA to break. An international team of paleogeneticists sought to measure the half-life of DNA. They published their results in 2012 in the journal *Proceedings of the Royal Society of London, Series B*.

To measure DNA half-life, the team examined 158 leg bones from different species of moa, extinct giant flightless birds from New Zealand, all found in the same region and all preserved under similar environmental conditions. The moa bones ranged from six hundred to eight thousand years old. The team drilled into the bones and measured the amount of DNA remaining in each. They calculated a half-life for DNA of 521 years. In that time, half of the nucleotide bonds in DNA are broken, and in another 521 years, half of the remaining bonds are broken, and so on. Since an animal's genome may contain more than one billion nucleotides to start with, the breakdown takes millions of years. After about 1.5 million years, the DNA becomes so decayed that scientists cannot read its sequences. After 6.8 million years, the DNA has completely decayed.

The 521-year figure is only an estimate of the half-life of DNA. The half-life varies from fossil to fossil, depending on the type of tissue. Environmental conditions such as temperature, humidity, and soil chemistry also influence how quickly DNA decays.

Dinosaurs became extinct sixty-five million years ago, so their bones are at least that old. A sixty-five-million-year-old fossil is far too old to contain any intact DNA. That is why we'll never see *T. rex* walking among us.

CHAPTER THREE

A PHOTOGRAPHER POSES WITH A MAMMOTH TUSK ON WRANGEL ISLAND IN SOUTHEASTERN ALASKA. MAMMOTH TUSKS, HAIR, SKIN, AND OTHER BODY PARTS ALL CONTAIN DNA. IT HAS MOSTLY DECAYED, BUT SCIENTISTS HAVE USED FRAGMENTS OF MAMMOTH DNA TO PIECE TOGETHER THE ANIMAL'S ENTIRE GENOME.

MAMMOTH 2.0

When woolly mammoths roamed Earth, their genome—their complete set of genetic instructions—existed inside the nucleus of every living mammoth cell, where it was packaged into chromosomes. But thousands of years have passed since the ground has rumbled with the steps of living woolly mammoths. Mammoth DNA still exists—within mammoth hair, bones, and other tissue—but it has decayed into fragments.

DNA starts to decay when an animal dies. Water, bacteria, and ultraviolet light from the sun can all damage and break DNA. Over time, what began as a long strand of DNA turns into smaller and smaller fragments. How quickly this happens depends on many factors, including the type of tissue, when and how the animal died, and what happened after it died. If its body lay exposed on the ground in a warm, wet climate, all of its DNA might have been destroyed in less than one year. But a body buried by windblown dust and soil in a cold, dry place will deteriorate much more slowly. The DNA might remain intact for hundreds of thousands of years.

Because woolly mammoths have been dead for such

a long time, their DNA tends to be severely decayed. The typical mammoth carcass contains DNA fragments of only about seventy nucleotides long. (An average intact elephant chromosome, by comparison, can be one hundred million nucleotides long.) But despite the high level of decay, the remaining fragments are long enough to be useful to researchers. In a fragment, the genetic instructions are still present, though in chopped-up form, and scientists can use the bits of broken DNA to reassemble the instruction manual.

In the first decade of the twenty-first century, Stephan Schuster and Webb Miller of Pennsylvania State University and Thomas Gilbert of the University of Copenhagen set out to sequence (read the arrangement of bases in) mammoth DNA. Gilbert decided to get the DNA from mammoth hair. He knew that hair is often a better source of DNA than bone, which is porous and soaks up contaminants, such as bacteria, like a sponge. But keratin, a protein found in hair, seals contaminants out "like a biological plastic," Schuster said. That leaves the DNA relatively uncontaminated.

The researchers obtained mammoth hair from museums and other sources. They even bought some from a Russian dealer on the online marketplace eBay. The samples ranged in age from twenty thousand to sixty thousand years old.

To piece together the mammoth genome, Schuster, Miller, and Gilbert first read the sequence—the order of As, Cs, Gs, and Ts—of individual DNA fragments. They used a technique known as next-generation sequencing, which enabled them to read millions of short fragments of DNA at one time. Once the team had read the bases for millions of fragments, they looked for places where the fragments overlapped. Science writer Carl Zimmer compares it to taking the popular cookbook *Joy of Cooking* and running it through a paper shredder. "Let's say that somebody for some reason decided to shred a hundred copies of the *Joy of Cooking* and threw them in the trash. If you took them home and were very patient you'd start to find pieces that lined up. They might overlap, and you could build out parts of the cookbook." That's what Schuster's team did with the overlapping pieces of DNA from different animals. They put the strands in order to form a complete genome.

In 2007 and 2008, the team published several papers describing its results. It wasn't the first time mammoth DNA had been sequenced, but this effort yielded far more of the sequence—four billion DNA bases—and demonstrated that it was possible to reassemble the genetic instructions for making a mammoth.

Since then other researchers have done even more complete and more accurate sequencing of the woolly mammoth genome.

EDITING THE ELEPHANT

Sequencing the mammoth genome is not just a nifty scientific feat. Some scientists say it could have real-world benefits to Asian elephants. These elephants live in India, China, and Southeast Asia, one of the most densely peopled parts of the world. In the twenty-first century, big cities, farms, and roads cover most of the land where the elephants once roamed. Only 15 percent of their original habitat remains. As the human population keeps growing, the remaining elephant habitat is shrinking fast. The animals are at serious risk of extinction.

That's where the mammoth genome comes in. A team led by geneticist George Church at Harvard Medical School in Massachusetts wants to use genetic engineering to produce Asian elephants with traits that helped woolly mammoths survive the cold. The genetically engineered cold-adapted elephants could live in the Arctic tundra, where few people live. With less human interference, the elephant population might recover.

Paleogeneticist Beth Shapiro explains, "Let's say all of the natural habitat for elephants disappeared. . . . We could use this technology [creating mammoth-like elephants]—not to bring mammoths back but to save elephants."

In 2015 a team led by Miller and Schuster compared the genomes of two woolly mammoths with the genomes of three Asian elephants. The team identified 1.4 million places where the two genomes differed, a large number of changes but not a surprising amount, considering the millions of years that have passed since the two species split off from a common ancestor. The team focused on around sixteen hundred mammoth genes that differed from elephant genes. To learn what these

As their habitat shrinks, Asian elephants are increasingly at risk for extinction. One plan to save them involves making mammoth-like elephants using genetic engineering. Elephants with thick layers of fat and heavy fur could live in the Arctic tundra, where few people make their homes.

George Church and his team at Harvard University are editing elephant DNA to make it more like mammoth DNA. An elephant with mammoth traits could survive in cold climates. Here Church shows a computer screen displaying a human DNA sequence.

altered genes might be doing in mammoths, they compared the mammoth gene sequences with massive gene databases, looking for similar genes with known functions in other organisms. The researchers discovered that mammoth DNA contained many genes that may have helped woolly mammoths survive in Arctic regions, such as genes that control skin and hair characteristics, fat, and temperature sensing. For example, they found that the mammoth genome contains extra copies of a gene that controls fat production, which could explain the thick layers of fat that helped woolly mammoths survive.

George Church's group wants to use this information to genetically engineer elephants with mammoth-like traits. The goal could be within reach thanks to a revolution that has been taking place in genetics. The roots of the revolution trace back to 1987, when scientists at Osaka University in Japan discovered repeating sequences of DNA in bacteria. Called *clustered regularly* *i*nterspaced *s*hort *p*alindromic *r*epeats (CRISPRs), the sequences have two parts: a protein called Cas9 that acts like scissors and cuts DNA, and a guide molecule that sends Cas9 to the DNA target. Bacteria use CRISPRs to chop up and remove harmful viruses that might invade them. The genetics revolution picked up steam in 2012, when an international team of researchers published a paper about CRISPRs in the journal *Science*. The paper described how CRISPRs could be used to edit any genes.

Biologists have long been able to edit the genomes of living things, but their tools were difficult to use, slow, and expensive. The new CRISPR-based tools are easy to use and inexpensive. Building on the new approach, in 2008 Church's lab invented a machine that sped up genome editing. With this machine, researchers could use CRISPRs to edit many places in the genome all at once. Almost overnight, editing the genomes of living things became cheap, easy, and fast.

Using the new technology, Church's team is tweaking Asian elephant genes to make them more mammoth-like. In the lab, researchers create synthetic (artificial) nucleotides, building fragments of DNA that match the woolly mammoth DNA sequence. They then splice (insert) that DNA into the genome of an elephant. In effect, they edit the genome, swapping out elephant genes and replacing them with mammoth genes. The team is starting small, editing a few genes in elephant cells and embryos. After each round of edits, the scientists evaluate the changes. They ask, "Did the edit produce a change in the physical characteristics of the cell or embryo?" For instance, when they edit a gene for hemoglobin, the protein in red blood cells that carries oxygen, they measure the ability of the edited cells to carry oxygen. Were they to edit a gene for hair production, they would have to grow elephant embryos to the point where the embryos began to make hair and then observe whether the hair was longer or thicker.

If scientists could find an intact mammoth cell, they could make a mammoth embryo and implant it into the womb of an elephant. Another cloning option involves altering the DNA of an elephant to make it more like mammoth DNA. The altered DNA could be inserted into an embryonic cell, also from an elephant, and a surrogate elephant mother would give birth to a mammoth-like elephant.

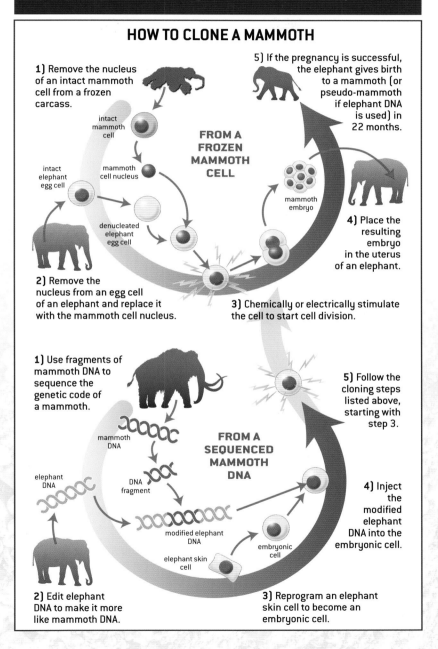

HOW TO CLONE A MAMMOTH

1) Remove the nucleus of an intact mammoth cell from a frozen carcass.

intact mammoth cell

mammoth cell nucleus

intact elephant egg cell

denucleated elephant egg cell

2) Remove the nucleus from an egg cell of an elephant and replace it with the mammoth cell nucleus.

FROM A FROZEN MAMMOTH CELL

3) Chemically or electrically stimulate the cell to start cell division.

mammoth embryo

5) If the pregnancy is successful, the elephant gives birth to a mammoth (or pseudo-mammoth if elephant DNA is used) in 22 months.

4) Place the resulting embryo in the uterus of an elephant.

1) Use fragments of mammoth DNA to sequence the genetic code of a mammoth.

mammoth DNA

elephant DNA

DNA fragment

FROM A SEQUENCED MAMMOTH DNA

modified elephant DNA

elephant skin cell

embryonic cell

5) Follow the cloning steps listed above, starting with step 3.

4) Inject the modified elephant DNA into the embryonic cell.

2) Edit elephant DNA to make it more like mammoth DNA.

3) Reprogram an elephant skin cell to become an embryonic cell.

None of this work involves live elephants, which themselves are endangered. Church's team takes elephant cells collected during routine veterinary visits and then cultures, or grows, them in a nutrient broth in petri dishes (glass or plastic dishes with removable covers) in the laboratory. "We're trying not to harvest eggs from Asian elephants or interfere with Asian elephant reproduction at all," Church explained.

Any animal that results from this work would not be a woolly mammoth—it would be an Asian elephant with edited, mammoth-like DNA. Some have called it a pseudo-mammoth. Others have suggested Mammoth 2.0. "I call them cold-resistant Asian elephants," said Church. "What the hybrid will be called will be up to popular decision making. . . . I'm not going to call them mammoths unless somebody insists. They're elephants with mammoth DNA."

ARTIFICIAL WOMBS

Critics of Church's work have pointed out that as the research progresses, at a certain point, Asian elephants might be put at risk. To create a cold-adapted elephant, an embryo would have to be implanted into the womb of a female Asian elephant. The surrogate mother would then carry the baby animal to term (until it was ready to be birthed). This situation raises serious ethical issues. Pregnancies can endanger a mother. Complications—such as the calf getting stuck in the birth canal—can lead to the death of the mother. Because of the inherent dangers of pregnancy and childbirth, the work could risk the life of an endangered animal for questionable gain.

Church is not deterred. He hopes to do the work in a way that never puts Asian elephants in harm's way. He imagines

THE ELEPHANT FAMILY TREE

Woolly mammoths and modern elephants are closely related. Scientists have long wondered which is the woolly mammoth's closer relative: the Asian or the African elephant? To find out, researchers drilled into a twelve-thousand-year-old woolly mammoth bone and extracted mitochondrial DNA, a type of DNA found in the mitochondria (the energy-generating bodies in a cell). They sequenced the mitochondrial DNA and compared it to that of modern elephants. The results: The modern Asian elephant shares 95.8 percent of its mitochondrial DNA with the woolly mammoth, while the modern African elephant shares slightly less, 95.5 percent. That slight difference reveals that woolly mammoths are more closely related to Asian elephants.

getting around the risks to elephant mothers by skipping the use of surrogates altogether. Someday, Church says, scientists might be able to take a baby mammal to term in the laboratory using artificial wombs. That would do away with the need for a surrogate mother. "I think it's worth a try to see if we can do it entirely without interfering with the reproduction of the species," Church says. "That may or may not be easy, but I think it's the ethical way to go about it."

Creating baby elephants completely in the lab? This approach sounds more like fiction than fact, but Church points out that researchers have already done this with mice, taking mouse embryos partway through their development outside the womb. In place of a womb, the researchers grew uterine tissue (taken from live female mice) in a laboratory dish, put mouse embryos on the tissue, and bathed the embryos in a nutrient-rich fluid. Mice embryos normally gestate (grow in the womb) for twenty-one days before birth. In this case, the embryos lived for seventeen days in the artificial womb but then died. Other researchers surgically removed a goat fetus from its mother at four months, about three-quarters of the way into the pregnancy. The researchers then grew the fetus in a fluid-filled aquarium outfitted with tubes that supplied nutrients, oxygen, and everything else the baby animal needed to survive and grow. A few weeks later, the researchers delivered a healthy, full-grown kid.

PLEISTOCENE PARK

To see where a cold-adapted elephant might live, the best place to go is Chersky, an Arctic town in northeastern Siberia. Three miles (5 km) outside of town, on a nature preserve called Pleistocene Park, a team of Russian scientists is trying to turn back time. They are re-creating the prehistoric ecosystem where woolly mammoths once roamed, the mammoth steppe.

The Pleistocene period began about 2.6 million years ago and lasted until 11,700 years ago. The Pleistocene included an

Scientists at Pleistocene Park say that musk oxen (*above*), cold-adapted elephants, and other grazing animals could help restore the mammoth steppe in Siberia and other Arctic regions. By grazing, knocking over trees, and churning the soil with their hooves, the animals would encourage the growth of new grasslands.

ice age that began around 110,000 years ago and also ended around 11,700 years ago. At the peak of that ice age, the world looked very different than it does in modern times. Around the world, temperatures were much colder. Ice sheets covered large areas of the planet, extending south of the Great Lakes in North America. South of the ice sheets was the mammoth steppe.

The mammoth steppe was the largest ecosystem in the world. It stretched across northern Europe, Asia, and North America, covering roughly half the world's landmass. The steppe was highly biodiverse and full of wildlife. Woolly mammoths grazed there alongside bison, horses, reindeer, musk oxen, elk, moose, saiga antelopes, yaks, and woolly rhinoceroses. Cave lions and wolves hunted among the herds.

The many grazing animals of the grasslands had a huge impact on the ecosystem. They ate an enormous amount of grass, stimulating grasses to grow new shoots to replace those that the animals had eaten. They fertilized the land with vast quantities of waste, turned over the soil with their hooves, and trampled seeds into the ground, promoting the growth of more grasses.

As the ice age ended, most of the grazing animals disappeared from the ecosystem. So did the grasslands themselves, to be replaced by spindly trees, bushes, moss—and few animals. The only herbivores (plant-eating animals) that could survive there were reindeer and moose. Some animals, such as mammoths and woolly rhinoceros, disappeared completely from the world at the end of the Pleistocene. Did the animals and their ecosystem both go extinct because the climate changed? Or were early humans to blame?

Russian ecologist Sergey Zimov is the leader of the mammoth steppe revival. He believes that as the climate warmed at the end of the Pleistocene, people moved north into the rich grasslands, which had previously been too cold for human habitation. Humans hunted the grazing animals, Zimov believes, and the herds dwindled. Eventually the number of animals dropped so low that the grasses that relied on the animals to fertilize and churn the soil could no longer grow. Forest and mossy tundra developed where grasslands had been. "The northern grasslands would have remained viable . . . had the great herds of Pleistocene animals remained in place to maintain the landscape," says Zimov.

If the mammoth steppe was destroyed by the loss of grazing animals, Zimov wonders if bringing the animals back could restore the ecosystem. Since 1989 Zimov, his family, and his colleagues have been testing this idea in Pleistocene Park. They have moved wild grazing animals—reindeer, moose, musk oxen, and bison—to fenced-in areas of the park that in some places are planted with grass.

The animals trample the ground, turning over the soil. The grasses they eat contain seeds. These end up in animal waste and embed themselves in the soil where the animals defecate. Then grass starts to grow in new spots. Across large areas that were once covered with tundra plants, the impact of the grazing animals is clear. Ungrazed land remains covered with mosses, spindly trees, and bushes—the plants of the tundra. On grazed land, the ground is covered with grasses.

The restoration of the mammoth steppe has gone so well at Pleistocene Park that the group has expanded its efforts at a second Russian site, called Wild Field. If the efforts continue, reviving the steppe over more and more land, the area could provide habitat to endangered animals such as wild horses, saiga antelopes, and Siberian tigers. It could also provide habitat to genetically engineered Asian elephants if they were successfully produced.

Woolly mammoths once played a key role in maintaining

MAMMOTH MISTAKE

The April 1984 issue of *Technology Review*, a journal produced by the Massachusetts Institute of Technology (MIT), carried an article titled "Retrobreeding the Woolly Mammoth." According to author Diana ben-Aaron, scientists had fused sperm from a male Asian elephant with an egg recovered from a frozen female mammoth, and the resulting embryos had been implanted into female Asian elephants. As ben-Aaron reported, "Most of the elephant cows [pregnant females] spontaneously miscarried, but two of the surrogate mothers carried to term, giving birth to the first known elephant-mammoth hybrids." The article said that the babies had yellow-brown hair and mammoth-like jaws and that they would be called mammontelephases, with the scientific name *Elephas pseudotherias*.

News of the scientific feat spread quickly. More than 350 US newspapers reprinted the article. Readers were shocked, especially in the era before the successful cloning of Dolly the sheep in 1996. When the newspapers reprinted the story, the editors had not noticed the day on which the original article had been printed: April 1, April Fool's Day! As the editor of *Technology Review* explained to readers in a later issue, ben-Aaron's article was a hoax. She had written it as an assignment for a college writing class, and the article was included in *Technology Review* in celebration of April Fools' Day.

the mammoth steppe. By inadvertently trampling bushes and knocking over trees, mammoths helped beat back encroaching forests. "Today we have no mammoths, so I use a tank [to do the job]," says Zimov. He bought the tank new and drove it to the park, over several hundred miles of dirt roads in the dead of winter. He uses the tank to knock down trees as a mammoth would have. Ultimately, Zimov and his team would like to raise cold-adapted elephants in the park. Elephants would knock over trees and help the grasslands expand without any assistance from humans.

CARBON BOMB

Elephants would bring another value to the tundra. Inner Siberia, where Pleistocene Park is located, is one of the coldest places on the planet. It is underlain almost entirely by permafrost. While the upper layers of soil freeze and thaw with the seasons, the permafrost underneath stays frozen.

Because of climate change, Siberia is warming and the permafrost is thawing. Locked in the permafrost are the roots of ancient grasses that have only partially decomposed. As the permafrost thaws, microorganisms will finish decomposing these long-buried plants. This will release huge amounts of carbon dioxide stored in the ancient plants. The buried carbon has been called a carbon bomb, one that could dangerously intensify climate change when the carbon emerges into the atmosphere. As much as 440 billion tons (399 billion metric tons) of carbon may lie trapped in the frozen Arctic soil.

Reintroducing mammoth-like elephants and other grazing animals to the tundra could slow the expected release of carbon from the permafrost and help offset climate change. In the absence of grazing animals, snow serves as a blanket that insulates the ground in winter, keeping it warm. Grazing animals trample the snow, and packed snow doesn't insulate as well as untouched snow, so the ground stays colder. If the ground stays frozen, ancient grasses won't decay and release carbon into the air. Zimov explains, "Introduce animals and they trample down that snow, looking for plants. Where animals graze, every single centimeter of snow is trampled at least once or twice a year and it loses its heat-insulating abilities. Pastures freeze so much more with animals present."

The hope is that cold-adapted Asian elephants could repopulate vast areas of tundra and forest across the Far North.

Global climate change is warming the tundra in Siberia and other Arctic regions. As the soil thaws, the roots of ancient plants will decay and release vast amounts of carbon dioxide, leading to even more warming. Scientists think that grazing animals could help the tundra stay cold by trampling snow and reducing its ability to hold in heat.

They would help revive the ancient grassland and help prevent the melting of the permafrost. It's an ambitious goal, and not one that would be quick or easy to implement. Preventing the melting of Siberian permafrost would require huge areas of tundra to be converted to grassland. As Beth Shapiro points out, "The challenge is going to be scale [the size of the project]. How much of this do you have to do in order to really impact the rate at which the permafrost is thawing?"

Such a project may never come to pass. But with human activities changing the climate and driving up extinction rates, scientists like Sergey Zimov and George Church are serious about de-extinction technology and the ways it could be used to benefit existing species and the planet. The question, says Beth Shapiro, is whether many people will get behind these ideas and make them happen. "What we need are big-thinking, world-changing, position-changing ideas in how we might slow climate change," she says. "Whether this [turning the tundra into grassland] is feasible would depend on a lot of people wanting to do this."

CHAPTER FOUR

THIS ILLUSTRATION FROM 1875 SHOWS HUNTERS IN LOUISIANA SHOOTING AT PASSENGER PIGEONS AS AN ENORMOUS FLOCK TRAVELS OVERHEAD. IN THE FOLLOWING FEW DECADES, THE SPECIES WAS HUNTED TO EXTINCTION.

THE GREAT PASSENGER PIGEON COMEBACK

On a warm spring morning in 1855, the townspeople of Columbus, Ohio, were going about their chores when they heard a low-pitched hum. Animals grew nervous. Horses tossed their heads. Dogs whined and paced.

Wispy gray clouds appeared on the horizon. People in the streets stood and stared. As the hum increased to a throb, more residents came outdoors to see what was the matter. They shouted at one another, over the noise.

The cloud grew and grew, and then darkness fell. The cloud had blotted out the sun. Horses bolted. Children screamed. People ran, women lifting their long skirts as they hurried indoors. A few people, thinking the end of the world had come, dropped to their knees to pray.

And then a cry went up from one end of the street. "It's the passenger pigeons! It's the pigeons!"

"LIKE METEORS FROM HEAVEN"

When European settlers arrived in eastern North America in the early seventeenth century, the passenger pigeon was the most abundant bird on the continent. An adult passenger pigeon was a little bigger than a mourning dove. The male had a slate-blue and gray head and a body with a coppery-purple throat and breast. The female sported drabber versions of these same colors. The birds' range extended from eastern Canada southward to lands that would become Texas, Louisiana, Alabama, Georgia, and Florida.

Their flocks were the stuff of legend. Passing flocks of passenger pigeons could blot out the sun for days at a time. The roar of their beating wings would drown out all other sound. Scottish-born ornithologist (bird scientist) Alexander Wilson, who moved to the United States in 1794, witnessed a passing flock on a canoe trip along the Ohio River between Kentucky and Indiana. He had paddled to shore to buy some milk and stood chatting at a farmer's door when the birds came. "I was suddenly struck with astonishment at a loud rushing roar, succeeded by instant darkness, which . . . I took for a tornado, about to overwhelm the house and everything around in destruction." To Wilson's obvious alarm, the inhabitants replied, "It's only the pigeons."

To Simon Pokagon, a nineteenth-century Potawatomi tribal leader, the birds elicited a sense of awe. "I have seen them move in one unbroken column for hours across the sky, like some great river," he wrote in the magazine the *Chautauquan*. "And as the mighty stream, sweeping on at sixty miles [97 km] an hour, reached some deep valley, it would pour its living mass headlong down hundreds of feet, sounding as though a whirlwind was abroad in the land." He continued, "Never have my astonishment, wonder, and admiration been so stirred as when I have witnessed these birds drop from their course like meteors from heaven."

Scientists have estimated the size of passenger pigeon flocks based on such observations. In 1860 a 1-mile-wide (1.6 km) flock in Ontario, Canada, left "the air filled, the sun obscured by millions of pigeons," according to one observer. The birds flew wingtip to wingtip, as far as the eye could see. The flock took fourteen hours to pass, which led the observer to estimate its length to be about 300 miles (483 km). Several scientists later used this observation to calculate the number of birds in that one flock. All arrived at an estimate of around 3.7 *billion* birds.

All told, scientists estimate that three to five billion passenger pigeons were on the continent when European explorers arrived. Because no one made scientific wildlife counts at the time, this number is just a guess. Still, based on the size of the flocks, it seems likely that the passenger pigeon was the most abundant bird not only in North America but anywhere in the world.

Yet the last passenger pigeon died in the Cincinnati Zoo in 1914. What happened?

WANDERING FLOCKS

Passenger pigeons were nomadic birds of the eastern North American woodlands. They moved from place to place, constantly searching for the best sites for nesting and feeding. Wherever they went, the birds stripped the woods of chestnuts, beechnuts, acorns, seeds, and berries. When the food in one area ran out, they moved to a new woodland.

Passenger pigeons also migrated with the seasons. They spent winter in the southern states, roosting so densely in the trees that branches sometimes crashed to the ground beneath their weight. Their clucking and chattering could be heard for miles. In spring they flew north and nested in dense flocks. At some nesting sites, which could stretch on for thousands of acres, each tree held more than one hundred nests.

Raising chicks took about a month: a few weeks for the eggs to hatch and then another two weeks during which the young pigeons, called squabs, lived under the care of both parents. Then the squabs left the nest, the parents flew off, and the squabs fluttered on the ground until they were strong enough to fly and join a passing flock of adult pigeons.

Scientists have speculated that because passenger pigeons gathered in such huge flocks, their habitat must have covered huge tracts of forest. When European settlers cleared eastern forests for farmland, the birds began eating newly planted fields of grain. Large flocks could seriously damage a grain field, and farmers fought back by shooting the birds.

But that was only the beginning of the slaughter of the passenger pigeon.

FROM BILLIONS TO ZERO

For the first Europeans to settle in North America, passenger pigeons meant food in lean times. The passenger pigeon's habit of living in dense flocks made them easy to hunt. So when a flock showed up, settlers knew they would have steady meals for a while. But even when other food was available, hunters still killed pigeons—sometimes more than could be eaten and just for sport. Alexander Wilson told of places where people ate pigeons for breakfast, lunch, and dinner for days on end. "The very name becomes sickening," he said.

In the nineteenth century, professional hunters began to kill large numbers of pigeons to sell as food in city markets. No laws restricted the hunting of passenger pigeons, and the newly invented telegraph—a network of wires for sending messages using electric currents—made it easy to spread the word. A message reading "the pigeons are here" would

go out, and professional hunters would hop on trains and head to wherever the birds were nesting. At nesting sites, hunters netted birds, shot them, and knocked young squabs out of their nests with sticks. They placed pots of burning sulfur under nesting trees, and when the birds—dazed by the fumes—fell to the ground, hunters scooped them up. They stuffed the pigeons in barrels and shipped them to cities, where they were sold cheaply, for about fifty cents a dozen.

By 1860 some observers noticed that fewer passenger pigeons filled the skies. But the hunting continued. At one nesting site in Michigan in 1878, hunters killed fifty thousand pigeons per day for nearly five months. When surviving adult pigeons tried to move to a new site and nest again, hunters found and killed them before they could raise any young.

By the 1890s, sightings of passenger pigeons in the wild had become rare. Conservationists protested that hunters were killing off the species. Some state legislatures responded by passing laws to protect the birds, but the laws were not enforced. By the first decade of the twentieth century, no passenger pigeons were left in the wild. The last two members of the species, George and Martha, lived in a cage in the Cincinnati Zoo. George died in 1910. Martha, the final member of her species, lived alone in her cage until her death on September 1, 1914. After her death, she was stuffed and

CONSERVATION LAWS

The slaughter and rapid demise of passenger pigeons created growing public support for strong conservation laws. By the end of the nineteenth century, other bird species had dwindled after being hunted to excess, but it was the disappearance of the once-abundant passenger pigeon that outraged the American public. In 1900 the US Congress passed the Lacey Act, the first far-reaching wildlife protection law in the United States. The Lacey Act made it a federal crime to take illegally killed game animals across state lines. Although the law came too late to save the passenger pigeon, it gave wildlife officials a powerful tool to protect other animals.

The US government passed other conservation laws after the Lacey Act. For example, the Migratory Bird Treaty Act of 1918 makes it illegal to harass, kill, harm, possess, sell, or trade any migratory bird—as well as any migratory bird part, nest, or egg—without a permit. The Endangered Species Act of 1973 gives the federal government the responsibility of protecting endangered and threatened plants and animals and their habitats. Once a plant or animal is listed as endangered or threatened, it gains federal protection and cannot legally be harmed, captured, traded, or sold. Those who break the law can be punished with fines and imprisonment.

The only passenger pigeons left are museum specimens such as this stuffed bird. Some de-extinctionists want to use DNA from such specimens to revive the species.

mounted. Her body resides at the Smithsonian Institution in Washington, DC.

Many mourned the loss of the passenger pigeon. In 1906 US naturalist C. William Beebe wrote, "When the last individual of a race of living beings breathes no more, another heaven and another earth must pass before such a one can be again."

"WILD SCHEME. COULD BE FUN."

The birds that once blotted out the sun no longer exist, except as specimens in museums and laboratories. Worldwide, these specimens total 1,532 passenger pigeons. Some are stuffed pigeons like Martha. Others are preserved in jars of ethanol.

Some collections include passenger pigeon eggs. Inside these specimens—in toe pads, feathers, and muscle tissue—is passenger pigeon DNA. Like the DNA in woolly mammoth fossils, it has been broken into fragments by decay. Could this DNA be used to resurrect the species?

Stewart Brand thinks so. In the 1960s and 1970s, Brand published the *Whole Earth Catalog*, an environmentalist magazine, and became a leader in the environmental movement. In 2011 Brand was thinking about the problem of mass extinction and became intrigued with the possibility of species revival. He felt that the passenger pigeon would make a worthy candidate for de-extinction. He wrote to George Church at Harvard University: "George, could we bring the bird back through genetic techniques? . . . Wild scheme. Could be fun. Could improve things. . . . What do you think?"

Church responded within hours, outlining a plan for a passenger pigeon revival. Soon after, on February 8, 2012,

Reviving passenger pigeons might involve genetically modifying band-tailed pigeons. A team led by paleogeneticist Beth Shapiro at the University of California has already sequenced the band-tailed pigeon genome.

Church chaired a scientific meeting at Harvard Medical School called "Bringing Back the Passenger Pigeon." Brand and his wife, entrepreneur Ryan Phelan, were there. So were ornithologists, ancient DNA experts, and bioethicists (people who study questions of right and wrong in biology and medicine). Everyone spent the day discussing the technical challenges—and also the consequences to society—of bringing back the pigeon.

On the technical side, Church presented a plan similar to the one his team is using to insert woolly mammoth traits into elephants. First, Church proposed sequencing the passenger pigeon genome and then editing the genome of a closely related bird to create a bird with passenger pigeon genes and traits.

After the meeting, Brand and Phelan created an organization called Revive & Restore. Its mission is "to enhance biodiversity through the genetic rescue of endangered and extinct species." They named their flagship project the Great Passenger Pigeon Comeback. The goal is to re-create passenger pigeons and rebuild flocks that, without human assistance, can survive and reproduce in North American woodlands.

PLAYING WITH PIGEON GENES

The passenger pigeon comeback starts with genetic detective work, similar to what has been done for the woolly mammoth. First comes sequencing the genome, using bits of DNA preserved in specimens. Beth Shapiro's group at the University of California has already done this work. Shapiro's group had also sequenced the genome of the closest living relative of the passenger pigeon, the band-tailed pigeon (*Patagioenas fasciata*), a bird common in the American West.

The next step is to compare band-tailed pigeon DNA with passenger pigeon DNA. By looking at the two genomes side by side, scientists hope to better understand what genetic distinctions gave the passenger pigeon its unique traits.

Ben Novak of Revive & Restore is leading the passenger pigeon project. His goal is to edit the band-tailed pigeon's DNA to make it resemble a passenger pigeon's DNA. Specifically, he wants to create the genes that gave the passenger pigeon its copper-colored breast, its nomadic habits, and its tendency to live in large flocks. Then he wants to use the edited DNA to grow a brood of birds that look and behave like passenger pigeons.

To do genome editing in birds, scientists must work with germ cells, the cells that will develop into sperm and eggs. Germ cells are present in young bird embryos, which grow inside eggshells. Using a process developed in chickens, Novak plans to remove germ cells from band-tailed pigeon embryos that have been removed from their shells. He will then grow and multiply the germ cells in a laboratory. The next step is to add passenger pigeon genes to the germ cells using gene editing by CRISPR. To get the germ cells back into a developing embryo, Novak plans to cut a window into another eggshell, inject the genetically altered germ cells into the bloodstream of the embryo there, and then reseal the shell. Although the process has not yet been used for band-tailed pigeons, Novak is optimistic that it will work because it has been done successfully in chickens. If Novak succeeds, the genetically altered band-tailed pigeon will then hatch, mature, mate, and—if it is a female—lay eggs. The offspring that hatch out of those eggs will carry passenger pigeon genes passed on by their mother. Different offspring from different mothers can then be bred with one another to produce birds with more and more passenger pigeon genes and traits.

Because the passenger pigeon is already extinct, Novak believes the stakes are lower than if his group were trying to save a species teetering on the verge of extinction. "If we succeed, the world gets a new organism," Novak says. "If we fail, we learn things that are valuable and the world isn't left with another extinct species."

A PLACE FOR PASSENGER PIGEONS?

If the genome editing work succeeds with passenger pigeons, Novak will continue heading into new scientific terrain. Reviving a genome is a far cry from recovering an animal's behavior, which depends on more than just genetics. Novak will have to reestablish flocks and teach them how to behave like passenger pigeons, particularly how to migrate seasonally and find food. And he will need to introduce the flocks into the passenger pigeon's old habitat in the North American woodlands.

In some ways, the United States has plenty of forest habitat for genetically engineered passenger pigeons. In 2016 the eastern United States had more forestland than it did a century before, when the passenger pigeon went extinct. But the makeup of the forests has changed. When the last passenger pigeon was languishing in her cage, a fungal blight (disease) from Asia was spreading like wildfire through eastern US forests. The blight killed off American chestnuts, which had been the dominant tree across much of the forests. Following the fungal blight, a series of newly arrived plant and animal species has continued to alter the makeup of eastern US forests. Some conservationists say that the forests are too changed to support revived passenger pigeons. Others say that passenger pigeons were adaptable birds and that new ones would thrive in the modern forests. The truth is, no one knows what will happen.

REVIVING THE CHESTNUT FOREST

Most de-extinction efforts focus on animals, but it is actually the restoration of a tree that is leading the way. When Europeans came to North America, they encountered forests filled with American chestnuts (*Castanea dentata*). These trees were both abundant and enormous, growing to more than 100 feet (30 m) tall, with trunks 8 feet (2.4 m) or more across. The American chestnut played an important role in the forest ecosystem, providing nuts to feed bears, turkeys, and a long list of other animals. In the early twentieth century, the American chestnut was nearly wiped out by a deadly fungus called *Cryphonectria*

North America was once home to vast forests of majestic American chestnut trees *(above)*. In the twentieth century, a fungal disease brought the American chestnut to near extinction. Botanists are using genetic engineering and crossbreeding with the Chinese chestnut *(facing page)* to create American chestnuts that can withstand the fungus.

parasitica, accidentally brought to North America on chestnut trees imported from Asia. Within eighty years, four billion American chestnut trees had died. In some cases, the roots of the trees survived and continue to live in the twenty-first century. These roots send up sprouts, but when the sprouts grow to about 10 or 15 feet (3 or 4.5 m), the fungus kills them.

In the 1980s, researchers began working to bring back the American chestnut. They have made substantial progress using two different approaches. First, they are crossbreeding American chestnuts with fungal-resistant Chinese chestnuts *(above)*. The goal is to create a hybrid tree that is genetically more than 90 percent American but carries the blight resistance of the Chinese tree. Second, researchers are genetically engineering the American chestnut, adding genes from other plants that give resistance to the fungus. After decades of research, both approaches are showing success, with new chestnut trees displaying much greater resistance to the fungus. The next stage will be reintroducing the chestnut trees into the eastern forests of North America. By the end of the twenty-first century, North American forests may again be filled with towering America chestnuts.

Novak believes that passenger pigeons were a critical species with a role in the health of the forest ecosystem. They fertilized the soil with their droppings. By breaking branches and toppling trees, they let sunlight reach the forest floor, enabling new plant growth. But bringing back those flocks could be a tall order.

Biologists have long believed that passenger pigeons needed to live in large flocks to survive. But creating such large flocks—which included millions or even billions of birds— would probably be impossible. Would smaller flocks do?

To find answers, biologist Chih-Ming Hung and his colleagues at National Taiwan Normal University in Asia obtained DNA from three US passenger pigeon museum specimens. Hung's team sequenced and compared the DNA of those three birds. In a paper published in *Proceedings of the National Academy of Sciences* in 2014, the scientists reported that genetic variation—the amount the DNA sequence varied from bird to bird—was quite low among the three passenger pigeons.

Low genetic variation is an important clue about the history of a species. It indicates that the population dropped in size at some point in the past. When many animals die, their DNA variations die with them. The surviving animals are not as genetically diverse as the previous population, and the generations that follow are not genetically diverse either. So the finding of low genetic variation among passenger pigeons showed that the species was "not always superabundant," says Hung. This finding agrees with Novak's own research into passenger pigeon DNA. He too has found that passenger pigeons were genetically a lot alike, suggesting the birds he studied were the descendants of birds that lived at a time when the passenger pigeon population was small. "All of our

Sometimes an animal or plant population drops dramatically in size—a situation known as a population bottleneck. The cause might be a severe storm, hunting, or habitat destruction. A bottleneck reduces overall genetic diversity, because when many animals die, their DNA variations die out with them. So after the bottleneck, the remaining population has very low genetic diversity. Even if the population recovers and grows in size, its genetic diversity will remain low. It can take tens of thousands of years for genetic changes to accumulate and restore genetic diversity—a key to long-term survival—to the species.

birds are all very, very similar to each other—like everybody being cousins, essentially," Novak says.

Scientists have found other signs that the birds didn't always live in huge flocks. Archaeologists (scientists who study the remains of past human life) have looked for passenger pigeon bones at prehistoric sites in North America. Surely, if the birds were present in huge flocks, they would have been an important source of food for American Indians, the archaeologists surmised. But rather than thousands of bones, archaeologists have found few traces of the birds at prehistoric sites. These results suggest that the population of the birds was small before Europeans arrived on the continent.

For Novak, all of this is a promising sign. He feels he may not need to re-create huge flocks to bring back the passenger pigeon.

SURROGATE FLOCKING

Another challenge to passenger pigeon revival is that birds (and many other types of animals) follow and mimic the behavior of their parents. This is called imprinting. Young birds learn other behavior, including where to migrate, how to find food, and how to raise chicks, from flocks of adults. But with no passenger pigeons in the wild, Novak will have to find a substitute to teach behaviors to the genetically engineered birds. He imagines using trained homing pigeons (a species that is easily trained) to act as "surrogate flocks." The homing pigeons could be colored with harmless dyes to look more like passenger pigeons and then be trained to ferry the passenger pigeons to designated spots.

The process would begin in protected, caged areas in US forests, giving the genetically engineered pigeons a chance to become acquainted with the forest environment. Then the birds would be released in the forest. The trained homing pigeon flocks could ferry the engineered pigeons around forests to find supplies of food and south to wintering areas. Then, gradually, researchers would remove the surrogate flocks.

Conservationists have gone to similar extremes to reintroduce other birds to the wild. Whooping cranes (*Grus americana*) are an example. They are the tallest birds in North America, standing nearly 5 feet (1.5 m) tall, with a wingspan of about 7.5 feet (2.3 m). Adult birds have snowy white feathers, a red patch on their heads, and a loud, clear call like the sound of a bugle.

Before Europeans arrived in North America, whooping cranes lived throughout the north central part of the continent. But as the European American population grew, the number of whooping cranes dwindled, largely because of hunting and destruction of the animal's wetland habitat, which people converted to urban areas and farmland. By the 1940s, the bird's population had reached an alarming low, with just fifteen whooping cranes remaining in the wild. Breeding and conservation efforts helped the whooping crane population bounce back, and by the beginning of the twenty-first century, it had reached 267 birds. But the whooping crane remained at high risk of extinction. All the wild birds lived in a single flock that migrated between Canada and Texas. Just one devastating storm could spell extinction for the entire species.

OPERATION MIGRATION

In 2001 the US Fish and Wildlife Service and the International Crane Foundation launched a program called Operation Migration. The goal was to introduce a second flock of whooping cranes—one that would migrate between Wisconsin and Florida—into the wild. First, workers raised whooping cranes in captivity. To avoid having chicks imprint on (trust and follow) humans and instead imprint on their own species, workers disguised themselves as adult whooping cranes. They donned baggy white costumes and used hand puppets that resembled the heads of adult whooping cranes to feed the birds.

With no wild flock in place to lead the young birds between Wisconsin and Florida, the researchers trained the birds to follow a small ultralight airplane. First, the birds learned to follow the ultralight plane as it taxied on the ground and later to follow it into the air. At migration time, a pilot flew the ultralight plane along the migration route and the young whooping cranes followed. "It was one of the most quirky, beloved and interventionist American conservation efforts," wrote the *Washington Post* in 2016. It was also expensive. The total cost through 2016 was $20 million. In 2016 the US Fish and Wildlife Service shut down the ultralight-guided migration because the project was not working.

The program had failed on many levels. By 2016 most of the whooping cranes in the second flock had died, from a whole host of causes. Blizzards killed some of them. Hunters shot others. Others died when they flew into power lines. The cranes did succeed in mating and laying eggs, but the adult cranes did not know how to care for their offspring, and many baby birds died in the nest. An even bigger problem was that cranes raised by people and then released into the wild lacked parenting skills. On the positive side, researchers learned a lot about whooping crane biology, and the project

In a program called Operation Migration, biologists taught young whooping cranes to migrate with the seasons. Because the cranes had been raised in captivity and had no adult birds to teach them, researchers trained them to follow an ultralight airplane. If scientists succeed in reviving passenger pigeons, the birds might need similar training.

drew attention to the conservation needs of these birds. Every year thousands of American schoolchildren followed the whooping crane migration online.

People aren't giving up on the whooping crane, but they are looking for new ways to boost its population. A new plan removes humans from the process, so that cranes can learn the skills they need to raise their young. In this plan, captive adult whooping cranes will rear chicks at Patuxent Wildlife Research Center in Maryland. Then wildlife workers will take the young birds to Wisconsin and release them to live with wild adult cranes that have demonstrated good parenting skills.

Although with mixed results, humans have gone to great lengths to save whooping cranes from crossing into extinction. To what lengths are people willing to go to bring back passenger pigeons?

CHAPTER FIVE

A RESEARCHER HOLDS A FEMALE SOUTHERN GASTRIC BROODING FROG AS IT GIVES BIRTH THROUGH ITS MOUTH. THE SPECIES, NATIVE TO AUSTRALIA, WENT EXTINCT IN 1983. SOME DE-EXTINCTIONISTS WOULD LIKE TO REVIVE IT THROUGH CLONING.

HOPES AND FEARS

On March 15, 2013, experts from all over the world gathered at National Geographic Society headquarters in Washington, DC. They were there for TEDxDeExtinction, part of a series of TED (Technology, Entertainment, and Design) conferences sponsored by the Sapling Foundation. As attendees settled into their seats, photos of endangered animals taken by wildlife photographer Joel Sartore flashed across the screen behind the stage.

One by one, experts took the stage. They discussed not only the technical challenges but also the ethical issues associated with bringing extinct species back to life. Mammoths and passenger pigeons got their turn in the spotlight. So did the bucardo, as the only extinct species actually to be revived. Michael Archer, a paleontologist at the University of New South Wales in Australia, described his group's efforts to resuscitate two creatures: an Australian frog that gave birth through its mouth, extinct since the 1980s, and the thylacine, or Tasmanian tiger, which went extinct in 1936.

THE FROG WITH A FROG IN ITS THROAT

The southern gastric brooding frog (*Rheobatrachus silus*) was a bizarre creature. It was discovered in 1972 in the mountains of Australia. It seemed to be just another frog until biologist Mike Tyler of the University of Adelaide uncovered the unusual way it reproduced.

Most female frogs lay their eggs in a pool of water. A male frog clings to the female, depositing his sperm on the eggs and fertilizing them as they leave her body. Both parents leave the eggs, which develop and mature on their own. The eggs hatch into tadpoles, and the tadpoles develop into adult frogs, all without the help of the parents.

The gastric brooding frog took a different approach. After a male fertilized her eggs, the female frog swallowed them. For six or seven weeks, her normal digestion shut down as the eggs developed in her stomach. The eggs became tadpoles, and the tadpoles developed into frogs—in her stomach. Her stomach swelled, and eventually she burped up the little frogs.

Just as biologists began studying this amazing animal, the gastric brooding frog vanished. Biologists last spotted the frog in the wild in 1981. Despite several searches, scientists never found another wild individual. When the last captive frog died in 1983, the species went extinct.

In 1984, just a year after the southern gastric brooding frog went extinct, biologists discovered a closely related species, the northern gastric brooding frog (*Rheobatrachus vitellinus*), living in an Australian national park. A year later, it too went extinct.

To paleontologist Michael Archer, the southern gastric brooding frog seemed like an excellent candidate for species revival. Archer got in touch with Mike Tyler, the University of

Adelaide biologist who had discovered the frog's unusual way of reproducing. Archer learned that Tyler had stored tissue from the extinct frog in a laboratory freezer.

Tyler passed the frozen tissue to Archer, and in 2011, Archer and his team began trying to clone the extinct frog. The scientists took fresh egg cells from a distantly related species (the great barred frog, *Mixophyes fasciolatus*). They removed the nuclei of those eggs and inserted nuclei from the extinct frog. The egg cells began to divide and formed embryos.

At the 2013 TEDxDeExtinction event, Archer took the stage and reported on his team's success with frog embryos. While they had made embryos of the extinct frog, none of the frog embryos had lived more than a few days. As of 2016, that's where the group's progress remained, with embryos but no live frog. Archer is working with experts in cell development to try to figure out why the embryos didn't survive.

FROGS IN TROUBLE

With amphibians worldwide in decline, Archer believes the revival of gastric brooding frogs is necessary. If his team can revive gastric brooding frogs, the de-extinction of that species could pave the way for other endangered amphibians. "This work will be relevant to the rest of the frogs around the world," said Archer.

In some ways, the gastric brooding frog is an excellent candidate for de-extinction. Scientists have access to a supply of frozen cells. Close relatives of the frog are available to use as a source of egg cells in nuclear transfer experiments. And unlike passenger pigeons, frogs don't need other frogs to teach them how to survive in the wild.

But in other ways, the gastric brooding frog is not a

good candidate. No one knows why gastric brooding frogs disappeared. In the southern gastric brooding frog's forest habitat, a small amount of commercial logging was taking place during the extinction. Biologists wondered if logging had driven the animal extinct. In the northern gastric brooding frog's habitat, forest fires were breaking out when the frog disappeared. Perhaps those fires were the culprit, biologists had thought.

In 2016 biologists think differently about the cause of extinction. They believe the culprit was the chytrid fungus, which had traveled around the world with the African clawed frog in the twentieth century. This idea creates a tricky problem. If Archer and his team succeed in bringing back the gastric brooding frog, where would it live? The chytrid fungus has spread to nearly every part of the world. If the fungus is indeed to blame for the extinction of gastric brooding frogs, a resurrected frog released back into the wild would surely be wiped out by the fungus again. What is the point of bringing back a species if it faces the same threats that wiped it out in the first place?

Archer believes the de-extinction work is still worthwhile, even if the frog could not survive in the wild. "We can ultimately fix the wild," says Archer. "Even if we had to maintain most of the world's wildlife in artificial environments, that would be a thousand times better than to let them slide off the brink [die out]." Archer says that the frogs could survive in captivity while scientists studied them.

Biologists are already rescuing other kinds of frogs from extinction by whisking them into captivity at zoos and other facilities as they disappear from the wild. The hope is that one day scientists will solve the problem of the chytrid fungus and be able to return the frogs to their habitat. But adding resurrected frogs to the amphibian rescue effort may not be practical. "Zoos are extremely limited in space," said Karen Lips, a biologist at the University of Maryland who works on conserving amphibians in the wild. "I can't help but think that we can't even take care of what we've got, and now we're going to invest in very expensive techniques to recover a handful of special-interest species that may or may not be able to survive in the wild on their own."

Nonetheless, Archer is pressing ahead with the de-extinction effort. "If we were responsible for the extinction of the species, deliberately or inadvertently," said Archer, "we have a moral responsibility or imperative to undo that if we can."

THE TASMANIAN TIGER

On May 13, 1930, Wilfred Batty and his family were eating dinner at their home in Tasmania, an island south of Australia, when his daughter spotted a thylacine—a doglike animal also called a Tasmanian tiger. The animal was prowling about the yard for chickens. The farmer and his son grabbed their guns, and the son shot the animal in the shoulder. Twenty minutes later, the thylacine died. No one knew it at the time, but it was the last thylacine living in the wild. Six years later, when the last thylacine died in captivity, the species went extinct.

The thylacine had a doglike head and dark stripes on its back like a tiger. But it was neither dog nor cat. It was a marsupial, an animal whose young are born in an immature state. Like other marsupials, such as kangaroos, thylacine moms carried their developing young in pouches attached to the front of their bodies. The thylacine once lived and hunted across Tasmania. But when Europeans settled on the island in the early nineteenth century, they brought sheep, which they raised for their wool, meat, and milk. Settlers killed thylacines, convinced the animals would kill their sheep. The Tasmanian government even paid cash rewards for dead thylacines. Hunted and trapped relentlessly by settlers, the animal went extinct.

Scientists frequently point to the thylacine as a candidate for de-extinction. Michael Archer began to think about resurrecting the thylacine after seeing a thylacine pup pickled in a jar of alcohol at the Australian Museum, where he was the director. In the first decade of the twenty-first century, he and his colleagues extracted DNA from the pup. They also extracted DNA samples from thylacine skins, teeth, and bones in the museum's collection. The effort stopped there.

If the project continues, the next step will be to sequence the fragments of DNA and use them to assemble the thylacine's complete genome. Then the challenge will be to use the DNA to create a living animal. One approach would be to clone the animal using a related animal, the Tasmanian devil, as a surrogate mother. Another approach would be to edit the Tasmanian devil's genome by splicing in thylacine genes.

The photo on the left shows a thylacine in a Tasmanian zoo in the early twentieth century. Thylacines went extinct in the 1930s, but the species could be revived using thylacine DNA from museum specimens. With cloning techniques, scientists could create a thylacine embryo and implant it into the womb of a Tasmanian devil *(right)*, a related animal.

DE-EXTINCTION CRITERIA

For scientists to consider an animal as a plausible candidate for de-extinction, that animal has to meet certain criteria. Revive & Restore has published general guidelines for considering which species are the best candidates. The guidelines ask the following questions:

- **Is de-extinction of the species possible?** The answer is yes only if a close living relative is available to serve as a surrogate parent and only if the extinction is relatively recent, within about five hundred thousand years, a limit imposed by the half-life of DNA. (No dinosaurs. They're too old.)

- **Can a large enough population be brought back?** The answer is yes only if the animal can be bred in captivity, if the original cause of extinction has been resolved (to prevent the species from simply becoming extinct again), and if habitat for the animal is available. (No Yangtze River dolphins. Their habitat remains polluted, and boats and dams on the river make it even less safe for dolphins.)

- **Should the species be brought back?** Answering this question involves ethical, ecological, and social discussions. Scientists have to consider whether the animal might carry disease or might endanger humans or other animals. (No saber-toothed tigers. We probably don't want them roaming in the wild, preying on elephants and other creatures that are already endangered.)

A MARATHON, NOT A SPRINT

The scientific community faces a number of major hurdles in pulling off species revival. De-extinction requires cooperation among researchers with expertise in different areas of biology. De-extinction—and, ultimately, reintroducing species into the wild—requires long-term commitments from governments, universities, wildlife organizations, and the public. De-extinction also requires money—a lot of it. Lack of funding is one reason progress on resurrecting the bucardo has stalled.

Species revival is a long race to run. DNA sequencing and genome editing are only the beginning. Next comes creating a living animal, usually by way of a surrogate. And to truly restore a population, researchers would have to build not just one animal but many. They would also have to build in genetic diversity, or small genetic differences among members of a species. Without genetic diversity, a disease might wipe out an entire animal population. But in a genetically diverse population, some members might carry genes that give them resistance to the disease, ensuring that it doesn't destroy the species completely.

Next, the animals must be raised and studied in captivity before reintroduction into their natural or reconstructed habitat. The study would help researchers understand what exactly the animals need for reproduction and long-term survival. Reproduction can take decades. Elephant mothers, for instance, gestate their young for nearly two years, and young elephants aren't ready to mate for another fourteen years after that. Even if reproduction is successful, the reality is that many species introductions fail for a wide variety of reasons. "The challenge of de-extinction is almost always framed in technological terms—can we bring back species?— but what will happen to the animals after they have been recreated has received comparatively little attention," notes science writer Brian Switek.

So species revival is a marathon not a sprint. A successful revival would likely take decades—maybe even a century or more—to complete for any given species. "Bringing back the mammoth means sustained effort, intensive management, and a massive commitment of conservation resources," writes ecologist Jacquelyn Gill of the University of Maine. The same is true for any species.

Governments, institutions, and the public can be fickle. Political candidates often vow to cut down on wasteful government spending if they're elected, and they might pull the plug on a species revival program, viewing it as lacking value. A university administrator might decide that space on campus used for an animal breeding facility should instead be given over to a new stadium, which would bring more revenue to the school. The public too can lose interest and turn its attention and support toward other, more pressing problems.

TECHNOFIX FOR EXTINCTION

De-extinction remains controversial. At the TEDxDeExtinction event, some experts questioned and even denounced the idea outright. Biologist Hendrik Poinar of McMaster University in Ontario said of the woolly mammoth revival, "A part of the boy in me wants to see these majestic creatures walk across the permafrost. But the adult in me wonders whether we should."

David Ehrenfeld, a biologist at Rutgers University in New Jersey, criticized de-extinction as a diversion from the difficult and successful work of protecting endangered species. "At this moment, brave conservationists are risking their lives to protect forest elephants from poachers [illegal hunters]. And we're talking in this safe auditorium about bringing back the woolly mammoth?"

Some of the fiercest critics of de-extinction have come from the conservation world. Stuart Pimm, an ecologist at Duke University in North Carolina, calls de-extinction "molecular gimmickry [trickery]" that does not address core problems in conservation. One of these problems is figuring out how people can coexist sustainably with wildlife so that species don't become extinct in the first place.

Some conservationists argue that de-extinction leads the public to believe that technofixes—or technological solutions—will magically solve all our environmental problems. "Technofixes for environmental problems are band-aids for massive hemorrhages [bleeding]," says Daniel Simberloff, an ecologist at the University of Tennessee. "To the extent that the public, who will never be terribly

A researcher in South Africa analyzes lion DNA from a blood sample. By editing DNA, we might be able to revive extinct species. But conservationists say that it's better to put money and energy into keeping species from becoming extinct in the first place.

well informed on the larger issue [of extinction], thinks that we can just go and resurrect a species, it is extremely dangerous. . . . De-extinction suggests that we can technofix our way out of environmental issues generally, and that's very, very bad."

Pimm charges that de-extinction is a seductive fantasy. "It is a fantasy that real scientists—those wearing white lab coats—are using fancy machines with knobs and digital readouts to save the planet from humanity's excesses," Pimm says. "In this fantasy . . . there is nothing involving the real-world realities of habitat destruction, of the inherent conflict between growing human populations and wildlife survival. [De-extinction might lead people to ask,] Why worry about endangered species? We can simply keep their DNA and put them back in the wild later."

Bringing extinct species back to life will require a great deal of money. Is it worth it when conservation efforts already suffer from a lack of funding? Many scientists say no. "It is much more sensible to put all the limited resources for science and conservation into preventing extinctions,"writes Paul R. Ehrlich, a biologist at Stanford University in California.

Another argument against de-extinction is that it causes animals to suffer. For example, somatic cell nuclear transfer can lead to birth defects and early death, as happened with the cloned bucardo. "Is it fair to do this to these animals?" Beth Shapiro asks. "Is 'because we feel guilty' [for having driven animals into extinction] a good-enough reason?"

Another worry is that bringing back extinct animals could harm people or other living things. A revived animal might harbor a dangerous virus that scientists aren't aware of, and the disease could be accidentally released into the world.

WHAT ABOUT NEANDERTHALS?

Neanderthals (*Homo neanderthalensis*) were close relatives of modern humans. Would it be possible to bring them back? The answer is yes. Scientists have sequenced the Neanderthal genome, and it was very similar to ours. Neanderthals even interbred with ancient people. If your ancestors are from Europe or Asia, between 1 and 2 percent of your DNA comes from Neanderthals.

Should we bring them back? Scientists and bioethicists say no. "Neanderthals were sentient [thinking] human beings," wrote Svante Pääbo, the Swedish biologist who led the team that sequenced the Neanderthal genome. "In a civilized society, we would never create a human being in order to satisfy scientific curiosity." What's more, the health risks are enormous. No one knows if it is safe for a woman to bear a Neanderthal baby. Cloning experiments in animals suggest that cloning people would not be safe and would probably produce a high number of miscarriages, stillbirths (birth of an infant that has died in the womb), and babies born with birth defects.

A more ethical approach would be to use genetic engineering to make a few Neanderthal cells. Studying the cells might help scientists better understand Neanderthals and could even offer insights into modern human diseases.

A scientist working for the National Geographic Society reconstructs the skeleton of a Neanderthal woman. Humans and Neanderthals descended from a common prehuman ancestor, and the two species even interbred in prehistoric times. Neanderthals went extinct about forty thousand years ago.

Or maybe the species itself would be an invasive species, preying on or taking over the territory of other plants or animals and driving them to extinction. Maybe it would simply be a pest, an argument often made about passenger pigeons. Based on passenger pigeons' past behavior, experts expect that genetically engineered passenger pigeons would descend on farm fields, leave droppings all over yards and city streets, and generally wreak havoc on modern life. Beth Shapiro asks, "Do you think that wealthy people on the East Coast are going to want billions of passenger pigeons flying over their freshly manicured lawns and just-waxed S.U.V.s?"

Some people believe that de-extinction is just flat-out wrong. They argue that scientists are "playing God" by trying to resurrect species. Paleontologist Michael Archer responds, "I think we played God when we exterminated these animals." Science writer Brian Switek adds, "Our species has driven others to extinction, and is having such a substantial impact on global ecology that the imprint of what we're doing today will be visible for thousands of years to come. We're already intervening and rearranging nature, intentionally or not." So humans have already "played God" by manipulating nature, too often with negative outcomes for other species. Advocates say that de-extinction could involve manipulating nature in a positive way.

CHAPTER SIX

THIS PHOTOGRAPH OF NOLA THE NORTHERN WHITE RHINOCEROS, RELAXING IN HER ENCLOSURE AT THE SAN DIEGO ZOO, WAS TAKEN IN DECEMBER 2014. NOLA DIED LESS THAN A YEAR LATER. SCIENTISTS HAVE SAVED SOME OF NOLA'S CELLS. THEY MIGHT BE USED TO GENETICALLY ENGINEER NORTHERN WHITE RHINOCEROSES, AN ENDANGERED SPECIES WITH ONLY THREE REMAINING ANIMALS.

THE FROZEN ZOO

On November 17, 2015, at the San Diego Zoo, an elderly female northern white rhinoceros (*Ceratotherium simum cottoni*) named Nola began showing signs of illness. She wasn't eating much. She became listless. A veterinary team began to watch her around the clock. On November 22, Nola's condition worsened, and the veterinary team made the difficult decision to euthanize her. With Nola's death, just three northern white rhinos were left in the world. That makes the northern white rhino the most endangered species on Earth.

As conservationists and animal lovers around the world were learning the news of Nola's death, Oliver Ryder and Barbara Durrant were already hard at work. At the San Diego Zoo's Institute for Conservation Research, Ryder is director of genetics and Durrant is director of reproductive physiology. Whenever an endangered animal dies at the zoo, researchers race to remove some of the animal's sperm or eggs and a bit of its tissue for future research and possibly genetic engineering. Ryder and Durrant obtained samples of Nola's cells. They attempted to collect egg cells, but because of her advanced age, her body no longer had eggs, so the scientists saved cells from her ovaries and uterus instead.

Nola may have died, but her cells live on, preserved in a bitterly cold place known as the Frozen Zoo.

BANKING ON THE FUTURE

The Frozen Zoo, which is part of the Institute for Conservation Research, is 30 miles (48 km) north of San Diego. It occupies a windowless room with a sign on the wall reading "Frozen Zoo." In the room sit half a dozen large metal tanks. At the bottom of each tank is a pool of liquid nitrogen. Suspended over the pool are towers of plastic boxes. Each box is filled with rows of plastic vials. Inside each vial is the tissue of an endangered species.

In all, the tanks at the Frozen Zoo hold ten thousand tissue samples from nearly one thousand different species. The samples include cell cultures (cells taken from animals and grown in the laboratory), eggs, sperm, and embryos. Another set of tanks in another building holds a duplicate set of all these cells. Having two sets of cells ensures that the tissue won't be lost if the power goes out for any reason. A power outage at one building would shut down the machines and thaw and destroy the cells.

As of 2016, only one of the species whose cells are in storage at the frozen zoo is extinct. That species is the Hawaiian po'ouli (*Melamprosops phaeosoma*), or black-faced honeycreeper, a bird last seen in the wild in 2004. Scientists expect that as the global extinction crisis intensifies, more of the species in the Frozen Zoo will join the po'ouli as extinct species. When Nola the white rhino died in 2015, her kind took one step closer to extinction.

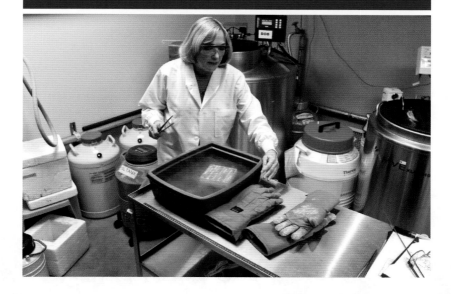

Barbara Durrant, director of reproductive physiology at the Frozen Zoo in San Diego, submerges animal cells in liquid nitrogen, which will keep them frozen indefinitely. The Frozen Zoo saves reproductive cells, somatic cells, embryos, and other tissues from many kinds of animals, some of them endangered or extinct. The cells might be used for artificial insemination, in vitro fertilization, cloning, or other procedures designed to increase animal populations.

The Frozen Zoo was founded in 1972, when researchers began collecting skin cells from rare and endangered species. Genetic technology was very new then, and the founders didn't know how the samples might be used, only that future scientists might find a use for them.

The Frozen Zoo is the world's oldest and largest frozen tissue collection, but other institutions have their own collections. The American Museum of Natural History in New York City has the Cryo Collection. The Cincinnati Zoo has CryoBioBank. The University of Nottingham in the United Kingdom has the Frozen Ark. All are saving tissues and DNA—collected from animals in zoos, captive breeding programs, and wild populations—in the hope that the material, if needed, could someday be useful to science, maybe even to save species from extinction.

THE BLACK-FOOTED FERRET

The black-footed ferret (*Mustela nigripes*) is an endangered species with low genetic diversity. Black-footed ferrets were once an essential part of the US prairie ecosystem, both as predators and prey. The ferrets mostly ate prairie dogs. In turn, larger predators, such as owls, badgers, and coyotes, ate ferrets.

In the twentieth century, US farmers and ranchers poisoned huge numbers of prairie dogs. Landowners viewed the prairie dogs as pests because they burrowed holes in farmland and ranchland and ate native vegetation. But without prairie dogs to eat, the black-footed ferret nearly went extinct.

Scientists thought the black-footed ferret was gone forever, but in 1981, they discovered a small population alive in Wyoming. At first, biologists took a hands-off approach, merely guarding and monitoring the colony. But the surviving ferrets, having gone through a severe bottleneck when their population declined, had very low genetic diversity. This made the colony highly susceptible to disease. When disease broke out in the colony in 1985, 22 percent of the remaining ferrets died.

In 1985 biologists launched a captive breeding program to save the species. They captured the last eighteen survivors and bred them using artificial insemination. In 1991 scientists began releasing the captive-born ferrets back into the wild, many of them in the western United States and Mexico. In the twenty-first century, black-footed ferrets now number in the hundreds. But their low genetic diversity still makes them susceptible to disease. De-extinction technology could help by restoring genetic diversity to the population.

In the late 1980s, scientists in the western United States saved black-footed ferrets from extinction using a captive breeding program.

Captive breeding programs have already used the tissue to help pull animals back from the brink of extinction. For instance, conservationists have used sperm from the Frozen Zoo to artificially inseminate giant pandas and other endangered species.

RHINO RESCUE

At zoos and wildlife parks, scientists use several techniques to breed endangered animals. The most basic is to put male and female animals together and encourage them to mate. Artificial insemination is another method. Neither approach is possible with the northern white rhino. None of the three remaining northern white rhinos, which live in a conservation park in Kenya, can breed naturally. Sudan, a forty-two-year-old male, has a low sperm count. His twenty-six-year-old daughter, Najin, has injuries that prevent her from mating or carrying a pregnancy to term. Her fifteen-year-old daughter, Fatu, has a uterine disorder that prevents her from sustaining a pregnancy.

Another option is in vitro fertilization (IVF). In this process, researchers extract eggs from females, fertilize them in the lab with sperm taken from males, and implant the embryos that result into the wombs of females. In 2016 a team led by San Diego Zoo Global in California and the Leibniz Institute for Zoo and Wildlife Research in Berlin, Germany, unveiled a plan to save the northern white rhinos using IVF. The scientists are collecting eggs from Najin and Fatu, the last two living females of the species, and fertilizing them with frozen sperm. They will implant the embryos they hope will result in a surrogate animal, the closely related southern white rhino (*Ceratotherium simum simum*).

With only two egg donors, Najin and Fatu, it will not be possible to create a genetically diverse northern white rhino population. Researchers will try to add diversity by turning frozen somatic cells saved from other northern white rhinos into stem cells, which can then be turned into eggs and sperm. Even if this succeeds, genetic diversity will remain low, since all the available northern white rhino cell cultures are genetically very similar.

Still researchers are hopeful. "Other species . . . have come back from numbers that small so we think there is good reason we can do this with the northern white rhino," said Barbara Durrant. But not everyone is a believer. Paul R. Ehrlich of Stanford University says that rather than genetically engineering endangered animals, the world needs to address

Park rangers and conservation groups sometimes intercept shipments of rhino horns bound for the black market. To raise public awareness about the illegal killing of rhinos and to prevent anyone from profiting from the horns, authorities sometimes burn them in big bonfires.

the root causes of extinction, such as human population growth and climate change. "Screwing around with science to save a white rhino might be fun and I would like to see it preserved and am all for biodiversity, but it's so far down the list of things we should be doing first."

So what should we be doing to save the northern white rhino? The animal's habitat is in war-ravaged African countries such as South Sudan and the Democratic Republic of the Congo. Governments there have been unable to prevent poachers from killing rhinoceroses for their horns, which some people—especially in China and Vietnam—believe are effective medicine. Well-armed poachers hack off rhino horns to sell on the black (illegal) market for large profits. They leave the animals to die. Journalist Peter Gwin says, "The slaughter has to stop if rhinos are to survive."

DE-EXTINCTION DREAMS

No animal can survive if it is hunted to excess. No animal can survive if its habitat is gone. Unless we work to save wild animals and their habitats, any effort toward de-extinction may be futile. We will revive species only to see them go extinct again.

The good news is that efforts to save animals and their habitats really do work. In a 2010 scientific paper in the journal *Science*, more than one hundred researchers assessed the state of the world's vertebrate animals. The researchers concluded that as dire as the extinction crisis is, many more species would have gone extinct without conservation efforts. They found that efforts to control invasive species and remove them from certain environments have been particularly effective. Fighting habitat loss has been less successful.

WHAT YOU CAN DO TO HELP

Want to help preserve biodiversity? You can begin right where you live. You can invite wildlife into your own yard or neighborhood by planting a garden to provide habitat for birds, insects, and other small animals. You can even declare your garden to be an official wildlife habitat, certified by the National Wildlife Federation. Learn more at http://www.nwf.org/Garden-For-Wildlife.aspx.

Another way to help preserve biodiversity is to volunteer as a "citizen scientist," assisting professional scientists in their research. Numerous US organizations are devoted to citizen science. Volunteers help scientists by observing wildlife, cleaning up waterways, and monitoring climate change. The work takes place in all sorts of settings, from city parks to rural fields and woodlands. You'll find information on a range of projects at http://nationalgeographic.org/encyclopedia/citizen-science/ and https://www.nwf.org/Wildlife/Wildlife-Conservation/Citizen-Science.aspx.

Jane Goodall is a world-famous primatologist—a scientist who studies animals such as apes and monkeys. Goodall's Roots & Shoots program gives teens a way to care for the environment in their own communities and around the world. Projects include planting trees, creating recycling programs, and building rooftop gardens. To learn more, visit rootsandshoots.org.

Zoos and aquariums are increasingly on the front lines of conserving wildlife and wild places. Many facilities rely on volunteers to help with their work. You can search for zoos and aquariums that need help by visiting https://www.aza.org/find-a-zoo-or-aquarium.

A teen volunteer cuts the ribbon at a ceremony marking the opening of a new tiger habitat at the Palm Beach Zoo in West Palm Beach, Florida.

The researchers noted that not enough area is devoted to wildlife sanctuaries and that management within these sanctuaries (such as work to prevent poaching) is often ineffective. Regulation of hunting and fishing has helped save some species, the researchers found, though many species remain in danger. The scientists concluded that current conservation efforts remain insufficient when stacked up against all the threats species face. If we want to save biodiversity on the planet, we must do more to stop the destruction of animals and their habitats.

Another huge problem that must be addressed is climate change. In a 2015 assessment of extinction risks from climate change published in *Science*, ecologist Mark Urban found that one in six species could face extinction if climate change proceeds as expected. Urban reported that species in South America, Australia, and New Zealand face the greatest risk of extinction, and the risks accelerate with each predicted degree rise in global temperatures. To limit global extinctions, the countries of the world will need to work together to limit climate change. The basic way to do this is to reduce carbon dioxide emissions, for example by switching from fossil fuels to nonpolluting alternative energies, such as solar and wind power.

De-extinction represents a new and different way to cope with extinction. For now, it is just a dream. No one has yet brought back an extinct species for good. Although the dream looks possible, whether researchers can make it happen remains to be seen. If they succeed, animals and ecosystems from the past could flicker back to life in the future. But even if that never comes to pass, scientists might still use de-extinction technology to help prevent extinction from happening in the first place.

SOURCE NOTES

7 Kai Kupferschmidt, "Can Cloning Revive Spain's Extinct Mountain Goat?," *Science* 344 (2014): 137–138.

18 "Why and Why Not Is a Matter of Specifics: Kate Jones at TEDxDeExtinction," YouTube video, 12:32, posted by "TEDx Talks," April 15, 2013, https://www.youtube.com/watch?v=EqEs-P_LvPs.

31 Jacquelyn Gill, "Cloning Woolly Mammoths: It's the Ecology, Stupid," *Scientific American*, March 18, 2013, http://blogs.scientificamerican.com/guest-blog/cloning-woolly-mammoths-its-the-ecology-stupid/.

35 Mason Inman, "Mammoths to Return? DNA Advances Spur Resurrection Debate," *National Geographic*, June 25, 2007, http://news.nationalgeographic.com/news/2007/06/070625-dna-resurrection.html.

36 Beth Shapiro, *How to Clone a Mammoth: The Science of De-extinction* (Princeton, NJ: Princeton University Press, 2015), 99.

40 Tom Avril, "Woolly Mammoths Provide a Gold Mine of Old DNA," *San Diego Tribune*, October 11, 2007, http://www.sandiegouniontribune.com/uniontrib/20071011/news_lz1c11mammoth.html.

40–41 Carl Zimmer, "Some Extinction Is (Not Necessarily) Forever," Long Now Foundation, accessed January 1, 2016, http://longnow.org/revive/.

42 "Is Jurassic World Closer Than We Think?," *Telegraph* (London), June 7, 2015, http://www.telegraph.co.uk/film/jurassic-world/pleistocene-park-dna-dinosaurs/.

46 George Church, interview with author, January 2016.

46 Lila Shapiro, "We May Resurrect the Mammoth Sooner Than You Think," *Huffington Post*, December 18, 2015, http://www.huffingtonpost.com/entry/woolly-mammoth-crispr-climate_us_567313f8e4b0648fe302a45e.

47 Church, interview.

50 Sergey A. Zimov, "Pleistocene Park: Return of the Mammoth's Ecosystem," *Science* 308 (2005): 798.

51 "Retrobreeding the Woolly Mammoth," Museum of Hoaxes, accessed February 3, 2016, http://hoaxes.org/af_database/permalink/retrobreeding_the_woolly_mammoth.

51 Adam Wolf, "The Big Thaw," *Stanford Alumni*, September/October 2008, https://alumni.stanford.edu/get/page/magazine/article/?article_id=31018.

52 "Is Jurassic World Closer?," *Telegraph* (London).

53 Ibid.

53 Ibid.

55   Joel Greenberg, *A Feathered River across the Sky: The Passenger Pigeon's Flight to Extinction* (New York: Bloomsbury, 2014), 54.

56   Ibid., 49–50.

56   Ibid., 53.

57   Ibid., 5.

58   Ibid., 70.

58   Carl Zimmer, "Century after Extinction, Passenger Pigeons Remain Iconic—and Scientists Hope to Bring Them Back," *National Geographic*, April 2013, http://ngm.nationalgeographic.com/2013/04/125-species -revival/zimmer-text.

61   Andreas Weber, *The Biology of Wonder: Aliveness, Feeling, and the Metamorphosis of Science* (Gabriola Island, BC: New Society, 2016), 275.

62   Nathaniel Rich, "The Mammoth Cometh," *New York Times*, February 27, 2014, http://www.nytimes.com/2014/03/02/magazine/the-mammoth -cometh.html?_r=0.

63   "The Great Passenger Pigeon Comeback," Long Now Foundation, accessed April 1, 2016, http://longnow.org/revive/projects/the-great -passenger-pigeon-comeback/.

65   David Biello, "Ancient DNA Could Return Passenger Pigeons to the Sky," *Scientific American*, August 29, 2014, http://www.scientificamerican .com/article/ancient-dna-could-return-passenger-pigeons-to-the-sky/.

65   David Biello, "3 Billion to Zero: What Happened to the Passenger Pigeon?," *Scientific American*, June 27, 2014, http://www.scientificamerican .com/article/3-billion-to-zero-what-happened-to-the-passenger-pigeon/.

68–69   Biello, "Passenger Pigeons to the Sky."

70   "How to Bring Passenger Pigeons All the Way Back: Ben Novak at TEDxDeExtinction," YouTube video, 15:02, posted by "TEDx Talks," April 1, 2013, https://www.youtube.com/watch?v=rUoSjgZCXhc.

71   Karin Brulliard, "Whooping Cranes Are Pretty Terrible Parents. Are Humans to Blame?," *Washington Post*, February 29, 2016, https://www .washingtonpost.com/news/animalia/wp/2016/02/29/even-people-in -crane-costumes-cant-teach-whooping-cranes-to-be-good-parents/.

77   Ed Yong, "Resurrecting the Extinct Frog with a Womb for a Stomach," *National Geographic*, March 15, 2013, http://phenomena .nationalgeographic.com/2013/03/15/resurrecting-the-extinct -frog-with-a-stomach-for-a-womb/.

78   Ibid.

79   Ibid.

79 Ibid.

82 Brian Switek, "The Promise and Pitfalls of Resurrection Biology," *National Geographic*, March 12, 2013, http://phenomena .nationalgeographic.com/2013/03/12/the-promise-and -pitfalls-of-resurrection-ecology/.

82–83 Gill, "Cloning Woolly Mammoths."

83 David Biello, "TedxDeExtinction 3/15/13 Meeting Report," Long Now Foundation, May 17, 2013, http://reviverestore.org/events /tedxdeextinction/tedxdeextinction-2013/.

83 Ibid.

84 Stuart Pimm, "Opinion: The Case against Species Revival," *National Geographic*, March 12, 2013, http://news.nationalgeographic.com /news/2013/03/130312–deextinction-conservation-animals-science -extinction-biodiversity-habitat-environment/.

84–85 Rich, "The Mammoth Cometh."

85 Pimm, "The Case against Species Revival."

85 Paul R. Ehrlich, "The Case against De-extinction: It's a Fascinating but Dumb Idea," *Yale Environment 360*, January 13, 2014, http://e360.yale .edu/feature/the_case_against_de-extinction_its_a_fascinating_but _dumb_idea/2726/.

85 Rich, "The Mammoth Cometh."

86 Svante Pääbo, "Neanderthals Are People, Too," *New York Times*, April 24, 2014, http://www.nytimes.com/2014/04/25/opinion/neanderthals-are -people-too.html.

87 Rich, "The Mammoth Cometh."

87 Carl Zimmer, "Bringing Them Back to Life," *National Geographic*, April 2013, http://ngm.nationalgeographic.com/2013/04/125-species-revival /zimmer-text.

87 Switek, "The Promise and Pitfalls."

94 Julie Watson, "Survival for Some Endangered Species Hinges on 'Frozen Zoo,'" *Washington Post*, February 17, 2015, https://www.washingtonpost .com/national/health-science/survival-for-some-endangered-species -hinges-on-frozen-zoo/2015/02/13/b79a579e-b201-11e4-827f -93f454140e2b_story.html.

95 Ibid.

95 Ibid.

GLOSSARY

adaptation: a change by which an organism or species becomes better suited to its environment. Species that cannot adapt to environmental changes might go extinct.

artificial insemination: the manual injection of sperm into the reproductive tract of a female animal. Scientists use artificial insemination to impregnate animals in breeding programs, with the goal of increasing numbers of threatened or endangered animals. Artificial insemination can also be used in de-extinction efforts using frozen sperm from extinct animals.

background extinction: the standard rate of extinction on Earth that occurs through ordinary processes of evolution. Background extinction is distinct from mass extinctions, times in Earth's history when large numbers of species have died out quickly.

bacteria: single-celled organisms with no inner compartments. After plants and animals die, bacteria might break down their cells and destroy their DNA.

biodiversity: the number of different plant and animal species in a place or region. Biodiversity is critical to healthy ecosystems, since plants and animals rely on one another for food, pollination, distributing seeds, and other biological processes.

bioethicists: scholars who study questions of right and wrong arising from advances in biology and medicine. Many bioethicists question whether humans should tinker with natural processes by trying to revive extinct species.

captive breeding: breeding animals outside of their natural habitat, in wildlife parks, zoos, or other facilities. Biologists use captive breeding programs to increase numbers of endangered and threatened animals.

carbon dioxide: a colorless, odorless gas that traps heat in the atmosphere. The burning of fossil fuels—coal, natural gas, and petroleum—has added extra carbon dioxide to the atmosphere and led to higher temperatures on Earth and in the oceans. Many animal and plant species are unable to adapt to the higher temperatures and have gone extinct or are likely to do so in the future.

chromosomes: structures inside cells made of deoxyribonucleic acid (DNA). DNA contains genes, which hold instructions for how an organism will function, grow, and reproduce. Different types of organisms have different numbers of chromosomes in their cells.

climate change: the warming of Earth due to increased levels of heat-trapping carbon dioxide in the atmosphere. The extra carbon comes from the burning of fossil fuels (coal, petroleum, and natural gas). Many animals have been unable to adapt to Earth's warmer temperatures and have gone extinct or might do so in the future.

cloning: the creation of an organism via asexual (nonsexual) reproduction. An offspring produced by cloning is genetically identical to its parent. Many plants naturally reproduce by cloning. Most animals do not reproduce by cloning, but scientists can clone animals in the laboratory using genetic engineering technologies.

conservation: careful preservation, protection, or restoration of natural resources, habitat, vegetation, or wildlife. Many conservationists focus on keeping threatened and endangered species from becoming extinct.

CRISPR (clustered regularly interspaced short palindromic repeats): repeating sequences of DNA found in bacteria. Bacteria use CRISPRs to chop up harmful viruses that invade them. Geneticists use CRISPRs to edit genes.

crossbreeding: deliberately mating animals or plants of different breeds or species. Many farmers use crossbreeding to produce crops or livestock with desirable characteristics. Conservationists use crossbreeding to create organisms that are better able to withstand environmental threats and thus might be saved from extinction.

de-extinction: using cells of extinct animals to produce new living animals, thereby bringing a species or subspecies back from extinction. Some de-extinctionists try to create hybrid animals by combining genetic material from extinct and non-extinct animals.

deoxyribonucleic acid (DNA): a molecule found in the cells of all living things. DNA contains the instructions for how each organism will grow, function, and reproduce. De-extinctionists extract DNA from extinct animals and manipulate it in the laboratory in an effort to produce living animals from species that have gone extinct.

DNA sequencing: determining the precise order of chemical units called bases in a strand of DNA. The sequence of the bases determines an organism's traits. Scientists have determined the DNA sequences of many extinct animals. They can use this information to create organisms that genetically resemble extinct species.

ecosystem: a biological community of living things and the environment in which they exist. When one member of an ecosystem becomes extinct, other members might suffer, because plants and animals within an ecosystem rely on one another for food and biological processes.

embryo: an unborn or unhatched offspring in an early stage of development. To revive extinct species, scientists use cells from extinct animals to create embryos. Scientists implant the embryos into the wombs of surrogate animal mothers, where the embryos can develop until they are ready to be born.

endangered species: a species that is at serious risk of extinction. Efforts to keep endangered species from going extinct include captive breeding programs, wildlife refuges, and laws that restrict certain human activities (such as hunting).

evolution: organisms changing over time, either randomly or in ways that enhance an organism's chances of reproduction and survival. These changes can lead to the development of different species.

extinct: having no living members. A species becomes extinct when the last individual of the species dies.

fertilization: the fusion of sperm and egg to form a fertilized egg, which will grow into an embryo. In most animals, fertilization occurs when a male and female have sex. Scientists can also fuse sperm and eggs in a laboratory to create embryos.

fossil: the remains or impression of a plant or animal of a past era. Some fossils take the form of rock. They develop when mineral-rich water percolates into dead plant or animal tissue, and the minerals gradually replace the tissue. Some fossils maintain the form they had when a plant or animal was alive. For instance, many fossils are animal bones or teeth. Fossils might also take the form of animal tracks or other impressions left in mud that has turned to stone.

fungi: organisms that obtain food by absorbing it from other living things. Fungi include molds, yeast, and mushrooms. Some fungi can cause diseases in plants and animals.

gene: a segment of DNA that contains information about a certain biological trait or function. For instance, certain genes gave woolly mammoths their thick layers of fat. Other genes gave them long, shaggy coats. Offspring inherit genes from their parents.

genetic diversity: variations in the DNA sequences of individuals in the same species. Without genetic diversity, a disease might wipe out an entire species. But in a genetically diverse population, some members might carry genes that give them resistance to the disease, ensuring that it doesn't destroy the species completely.

genetic engineering: the deliberate modification of the characteristics of a living thing by manipulating its DNA. In de-extinction, genetic engineering includes fusing the cells of extinct animals with cells of living animals and altering the DNA of living animals to make it resemble the DNA of extinct animals.

genetics: the study of heredity, or the passing of genes from one generation to the next

genome: a complete set of information about the genetic material of a cell or an organism. The human genome has around three billion bases and about thirty thousand genes. Even fairly simple insects can have large genomes. For example, many kinds of insects have more DNA than humans do.

germ cell: a sperm cell or an egg cell. When a sperm cell fertilizes (fuses with) an egg cell, the fertilized egg cell grows into an embryo.

habitat: the natural home—such as a desert, mountain, or lake—of a living thing. Habitats provide plants and animals with everything they need for survival, such as food, shelter, protection, and mating partners.

half-life: the time it takes for half of a certain amount of a material to decay or break down through natural processes. The half-life of DNA is about 521 years. It takes this long for half of the nucleotide bonds in a given amount of DNA to break. As DNA breaks down, it becomes harder for geneticists to sequence.

hybrid: the offspring of two plants or animals of different species that have mated with each other. Some de-extinctionists want to create hybrids by combining genetic material from extinct animals and living animals with similar genomes.

ice ages: times in Earth's history when large areas of the globe were covered with ice sheets. The most recent ice age began about 110,000 years ago and ended about 11,700 years ago. At the end of the last ice age, many animals, including woolly mammoths, went extinct.

implantation: the process by which a fertilized egg becomes attached to the wall of the uterus at the start of pregnancy in a mammal. Implantation usually occurs naturally after fertilization. Scientists can also surgically implant fertilized eggs into mammals' uteruses in a lab setting.

imprint: to learn basic skills rapidly and early in the life cycle. Birds imprint by mimicking the behavior of their parents and other adult birds. For instance, they learn where to find food, where to migrate, and how to raise chicks.

invasive species: plants, animals, or other organisms that are not native to an ecosystem and whose introduction causes harm. Invasive species might prey on native species, consume all the available food, or spread diseases to native species. Many invasive species have led to the extinction of native species.

in vitro fertilization (IVF): a process by which doctors or other scientists remove mature eggs from a female's reproductive tract, fertilize them in a laboratory using sperm collected from a male, and implant them into the womb of the first female or of a surrogate mother. Conservationists sometimes use in vitro fertilization to impregnate female animals of endangered species.

mammals: warm-blooded vertebrates (animals with backbones) that possess hair or fur and that nourish their young with milk produced by mammary glands. Humans are mammals, as are sheep, goats, and elephants.

mass extinction: a widespread extinction of living things that takes place during a relatively short amount of time. Earth has experienced five mass extinctions in its history, and many scientists believe that human activities are causing a sixth extinction in modern times.

natural selection: the process, first proposed by British naturalist Charles Darwin in 1859, by which organisms that are best adapted to their environment are more likely to survive and produce offspring. For instance, in cold places, animals with thick coats of fur are more likely to survive and have offspring than those with thin coats of fur. Those with thin coats might die out, while those with thick coats will pass on this trait to their offspring, which will also be more likely to survive and have offspring. Over the generations, the animals with thick coats will breed, and more and more animals of the species will have thick coats.

nuclei: structures in the cells of many living things that contain the genetic material, such as chromosomes and genes. In one type of cloning, scientists replace the nucleus of an animal's egg cell with the nucleus of a somatic (nonreproductive) cell from another animal.

nucleotide: a chemical compound that forms the basic building block of DNA. The arrangement of nucleotides in a DNA molecule resembles a twisted rope ladder. Nucleotides form the strands of the ladder, and sections of nucleotides called bases form the rungs of the ladder. The bases are adenine, guanine, thymine, and cytosine, designated by the letters: A, G, T, and C. The sequence, or arrangement, of the bases in DNA determines an organism's traits.

permafrost: a layer of permanently frozen soil underlying much of the land in Arctic regions. The frozen soil has preserved millions of carcasses of ancient woolly mammoths. With climate change, however, the permafrost is melting, which is expected to release vast amounts of carbon dioxide into the atmosphere.

poacher: a person who illegally hunts, kills, or captures wild animals. Poaching has led to the extinction of many animal species.

population bottleneck: a sharp drop in the size of an animal or plant population. A population bottleneck reduces genetic diversity, because when many members of a species die, much DNA variation is lost. After the bottleneck, the remaining population has very low genetic diversity.

proteins: large biological molecules that perform many functions for living things, such as providing energy to the body, carrying oxygen, and repairing tissue

somatic cell: any cell of a multicellular organism other than sperm or egg cells (germ cells). Some cloning techniques involve fusing a somatic cell from one animal with an egg cell from another animal.

somatic cell nuclear transfer (SCNT): also called nuclear transfer; a laboratory technique for creating an egg cell with its nucleus taken from a somatic cell of a different animal. SCNT is one method scientists use in cloning.

species: a group of living things of the same type. Male and female members of the same species can breed (produce offspring) with one another.

stem cell: cells found in embryos. Stem cells have the ability to turn into many different somatic (nonreproductive) cell types. In the first decade of the twenty-first century, scientists figured out how to turn somatic cells back into stem cells. They could then create embryos to reproduce extinct or endangered animals.

subspecies: a subdivision of a species, also called a variety. Members of subspecies differ slightly from other plants or animals in their species. They can breed with members of other varieties within the species but usually don't do so in the wild.

surrogate: a female animal that bears the offspring of another animal of the same or a related species. De-extinctionists might use a surrogate to gestate (carry to term) an embryo produced via cloning. Conservationists might use a surrogate to gestate an embryo produced by in vitro fertilization.

threatened species: a plant or animal species that is abundant in some places but might be at risk of becoming endangered

transcription factors: proteins that bind to DNA and turn on or off groups of genes. Scientists can use transcription factors to turn somatic cells back into stem cells.

tundra: a treeless region of northern Europe, Asia, or North America in which the soil is permanently frozen. Mosses and small shrubs are among the few types of plants that grow in the tundra.

viruses: infectious particles that are smaller than bacteria and that can cause diseases in living organisms

SELECTED BIBLIOGRAPHY

"Asian Elephants." World Wildlife Fund. Accessed March 26, 2016. http://wwf
.panda.org/what_we_do/endangered_species/elephants/asian_elephants/.

Avril, Tom. "Woolly Mammoths Provide a Gold Mine of Old DNA." *San Diego Tribune*, October 11, 2007. http://www.sandiegouniontribune.com
/uniontrib/20071011/news_lz1c11mammoth.html.

Beebe, William. *The Bird: Its Form and Function*. Charleston, SC: Nabu, 2010.

Biello, David. "Ancient DNA Could Return Passenger Pigeons to the Sky."
Scientific American, August 29, 2014. http://www.scientificamerican.com
/article/ancient-dna-could-return-passenger-pigeons-to-the-sky/.

———. "Conservation Works: Falcons, Ferrets, and Forests Benefit from
Preservation Efforts." *Scientific American*, August 9, 2007. http://www
.scientificamerican.com/article/conservation-works-falcon-ferrets-forests
-benefit/.

———. "Fact or Fiction? Mammoths Can Be Brought Back from Extinction."
Scientific American, June 10, 2014. http://www.scientificamerican.com
/article/fact-or-fiction-mammoths-can-be-brought-back-from-extinction/.

———. "TedxDeExtinction 3/15/13 Meeting Report." Long Now Foundation, May
17, 2013. http://reviverestore.org/events/tedxdeextinction/tedxdeextinction
-2013/.

———. "3 Billion to Zero: What Happened to the Passenger Pigeon?" *Scientific
American*, June 27, 2014. http://www.scientificamerican.com/article/3
-billion-to-zero-what-happened-to-the-passenger-pigeon/.

"Black-Footed Ferret Recovery Program." National Black-Footed Ferret
Conservation Center. Accessed July 5, 2014. http://www.blackfootedferret
.org/home.

Callaway, Ewen. "Mammoth Genes Provide Recipe for Creating Arctic
Elephants." *Nature* 521 (2015):18–19.

Ciszek, Deborah. "Elephas Maximus: Asiatic Elephant." Animal Diversity Web.
Accessed April 3, 2016. http://animaldiversity.org/accounts/Elephas
_maximus/.

"Clone Plan for Extinct Goat." *BBC News*. Accessed April 8, 2016. http://news
.bbc.co.uk/2/hi/science/nature/598799.stm.

"Columbian Mammoth and Channel Island Mammoth." San Diego Zoo.
Accessed April 7, 2016. http://library.sandiegozoo.org/factsheets/_extinct
/mammoth/mammoth.htm.

"Correcting Common Misconceptions about Mass Extinctions." *Understanding
Evolution*. Accessed March 10, 2016. http://evolution.berkeley.edu
/evolibrary/article/0_0_0/massextinct_05.

Cossins, Dan. "Half-Life of DNA Revealed." *Scientist*, October 11, 2012. http://www.the-scientist.com/?articles.view/articleNo/32799/title/Half-Life-of-DNA-Revealed/.

"Critically Endangered Northern White Rhinoceros, Nola, Dies at San Diego Zoo Safari Park." San Diego Zoo, November 22, 2015. http://blogs.sandiegozoo.org/2015/11/22/critically-endangered-northern-white-rhinoceros-nola-dies-at-san-diego-zoo-safari-park/.

Dankosky, John. "Project Seeks to Bring Extinct Species Back." *National Public Radio*, March 22, 2013. http://www.npr.org/2013/03/22/175054279/project-seeks-to-bring-extinct-species-back-to-life.

Dell'Amore, Christine. "Death of Rare White Rhino Leaves 5 in the World." *National Geographic*, December 17, 2014. http://news.nationalgeographic.com/news/2014/12/141216-rhinoceros-death-breeding-science-world-endangered-animals/.

Ehrlich, Paul R. "The Case against De-Extinction: It's a Fascinating but Dumb Idea." *Environment 360*, January 13, 2014. http://e360.yale.edu/feature/the_case_against_de-extinction_its_a_fascinating_but_dumb_idea/2726/.

"Endangered Species Act." US Fish and Wildlife Service. Accessed April 13, 2016. http://www.fws.gov/international/laws-treaties-agreements/us-conservation-laws/endangered-species-act.html.

Evans, Ondine. "The Thylacine." Australian Museum. Accessed April 3, 2016. http://australianmuseum.net.au/the-thylacine.

"The Extinction Crisis." Center for Biological Diversity. Accessed March 11, 2016. http://www.biologicaldiversity.org/programs/biodiversity/elements_of_biodiversity/extinction_crisis/.

"Feds to End Ultralight Aircraft-Led Whooping Crane Migration." *Chicago Tribune*, January 24, 2016. http://www.chicagotribune.com/news/nationworld/ct-whooping-crane-migration-20160124-story.html.

Fernández-Arias, Alberto. "The First De-extinction." TEDxDeExtinction. Accessed February 19, 2016. http://longnow.org/revive/events/tedxdeextinction/the-first-de-extinction/.

"First Comprehensive Analysis of the Woolly Mammoth Genome Completed." University of Chicago Medical Center, July 2, 2015. http://www.uchospitals.edu/news/2015/20150702-lynch.html.

Fisher, Pat. "Nation Marks Lacey Act Centennial, 100 Years of Federal Wildlife Management." US Fish and Wildlife Service, May 30, 2000. http://www.fws.gov/pacific/news/2000/2000-98.htm.

Gannon, Megan. "'Jurassic Park' May Be Impossible, but Dino DNA Lasts Longer Than Thought." *Live Science*, October 10, 2012. http://www.livescience.com/23861-fossil-dna-half-life.html.

Ghose, Tia. "Fresh Mammoth Carcass from Siberia Holds Many Secrets." *Scientific American*, November 17, 2014. http://www.scientificamerican.com/article/fresh-mammoth-carcass-from-siberia-holds-many-secrets/.

Gilbert, M. Thomas. "Whole-Genome Shotgun Sequencing of Mitochondria from Ancient Hair Shafts." *Science* 317, no. 5846 (2007):1927–1930.

Gill, Jacquelyn. "Cloning Woolly Mammoths: It's the Ecology, Stupid." *Scientific American*, March 18, 2013. http://blogs.scientificamerican.com/guest-blog/cloning-woolly-mammoths-its-the-ecology-stupid/.

"The Great Passenger Pigeon Comeback." Long Now Foundation. Accessed April 1, 2016. http://longnow.org/revive/projects/the-great-passenger-pigeon-comeback/.

Harris, Paul. "The Frozen Zoo Aiming to Bring Endangered Species Back from the Brink." *Guardian* (US ed.), August 28, 2010. http://www.theguardian.com/environment/2010/aug/29/frozen-zoo-san-diego-rhino.

"Homo Sapiens." National Museum of Natural History. Accessed March 10, 2016. http://humanorigins.si.edu/evidence/human-fossils/species/homo-sapiens.

Inman, Mason. "Mammoths to Return? DNA Advances Spur Resurrection Debate." *National Geographic*, June 25, 2007. http://news.nationalgeographic.com/news/2007/06/070625-dna-resurrection.html.

"Is Jurassic World Closer Than We Think?" *Telegraph* (London), June 7, 2015. http://www.telegraph.co.uk/film/jurassic-world/pleistocene-park-dna-dinosaurs/.

Jabr, Ferris. "Will Cloning Ever Save Endangered Animals?" *Scientific American*, March 22, 2013. http://www.scientificamerican.com/article/cloning-endangered-animals/.

Kearns, Carol Ann. "Conservation of Biodiversity." *Nature Education Knowledge* 3, no. 10 (2010): 7.

Kolbert, Elizabeth. *The Sixth Extinction: An Unnatural History*. New York: Henry Holt, 2014.

Kriger, Kerry. "Chytrid Fungus." Save the Frogs. Accessed March 19, 2016. http://www.savethefrogs.com/threats/chytrid/.

Kupferschmidt, Kai. "Can Cloning Revive Spain's Extinct Mountain Goat?" *Science* 344 (2014): 137–138.

Lee, Jane J. "African Clawed Frog Spreads Deadly Amphibian Fungus." *National Geographic*, May 16, 2013. http://news.nationalgeographic.com/news/2013/13/130515-chytrid-fungus-origin-african-clawed-frog-science/.

Lewis, Tanya. "Incredible Technology: How to Bring Extinct Animals Back to Life." *Live Science*, August 19, 2013. http://www.livescience.com/38972-how-to-resurrect-extinct-animals.html.

Maguire, Kaitlin. "The Elephantidae: Elephants and Mammoths." University of California Museum of Paleontology. Accessed December 10, 2015. http://www.ucmp.berkeley.edu/mammal/mesaxonia/elephantidae.php.

"Mass Extinction." American Museum of Natural History. Accessed January 29, 2016. http://www.amnh.org/exhibitions/dinosaurs-ancient-fossils-new-discoveries/extinction/mass-extinction.

"Mass Extinctions." *National Geographic*. Accessed January 29, 2016. http://science.nationalgeographic.com/science/prehistoric-world/mass-extinction/.

"Mission/History." American Chestnut Foundation. Accessed April 13, 2016. http://www.acf.org/mission_history.php.

"Nola, the Northern White Rhino, Leaves an Immeasurable Legacy through Her Contributions to Science." San Diego Zoo, November 24, 2015. http://blogs.sandiegozoo.org/2015/11/24/nola-the-northern-white-rhino-leaves-an-immeasurable-legacy-through-her-contributions-to-science/.

Novak, Ben. "Why Birds Are a Challenge." Long Now Foundation. Accessed April 14, 2016. http://reviverestore.org/why-birds-are-a-challenge/.

O'Connor, M. R. *Resurrection Science: Conservation, De-extinction and the Precarious Future of Wild Things*. New York: St. Martin's, 2015.

O'Neill, Tom. "Why African Rhinos Are Facing a Crisis." *National Geographic*, February 27, 2013. http://news.nationalgeographic.com/news/2013/02/130227-rhino-horns-poaching-south-africa-iucn/.

Pääbo, Svante. "Neanderthals Are People, Too." *New York Times*, April 24, 2014. http://www.nytimes.com/2014/04/25/opinion/neanderthals-are-people-too.html.

"The Passenger Pigeon." Smithsonian Institution. Accessed March 4, 2016. http://www.si.edu/Encyclopedia_SI/nmnh/passpig.htm.

Pearse, D. Colbron. "History: Persecution," 10, *Natural Worlds*. Accessed April 3, 2016. http://www.naturalworlds.org/thylacine/history/persecution/persecution_10.htm.

Pimm, Stuart. "Opinion: The Case against Species Revival." *National Geographic*, March 12, 2013. http://news.nationalgeographic.com/news/2013/03/130312–deextinction-conservation-animals-science-extinction-biodiversity-habitat-environment/.

"Pleistocene Park and the Northeast Science Station." Pleistocene Park. Accessed April 3, 2016. http://www.pleistocenepark.ru/en/.

"Population Bottleneck." Scitable. Accessed April 9, 2016. http://www.nature.com/scitable/definition/population-bottleneck-300.

"PSU Team Studies Mammoth Hairs." *Daily Collegian*, October 3, 2007. http://www.collegian.psu.edu/archives/article_b7799f9b-4b38-51fe-8047-e38d30a2c70a.html.

"Retrobreeding the Woolly Mammoth." Museum of Hoaxes. Accessed February 3, 2016. http://hoaxes.org/af_database/permalink/retrobreeding_the _woolly_mammoth.

"Revival Criteria." Long Now Foundation. Accessed April 1, 2016. http:// longnow.org/revive/candidates/revival-criteria/.

Rich, Nathaniel. "The Mammoth Cometh." *New York Times*, February 27, 2014. http://www.nytimes.com/2014/03/02/magazine/the-mammoth-cometh .html?_r=0.

Rincon, Paul. "Fresh Effort to Clone Extinct Animal." *BBC News*, November 22, 2013. http://www.bbc.com/news/science-environment-25052233.

Rutherford, Adam. *Creation: How Science Is Reinventing Life Itself*. New York: Penguin, 2014.

"Scientists Produce Cloned Embryos of Extinct Frogs." University of New South Wales, March 15, 2013. http://newsroom.unsw.edu.au/news/science /scientists-produce-cloned-embryos-extinct-frog.

Shapiro, Beth. "Mammoth 2.0: Will Genome Engineering Resurrect Extinct Species?" *Genome Biology* 16 (2015): 228.

Shapiro, Lila. "We May Resurrect the Mammoth Sooner Than You Think." *Huffington Post*, December 18, 2015. http://www.huffingtonpost.com/entry /woolly-mammoth-crispr-climate_us_567313f8e4b0648fe302a45e.

Sherkow, Jacob S., and Henry T. Greely. "What If Extinction Is Not Forever?" *Science* 340 (2013): 32–33.

Shreeve, Jamie. "Species Revival: Should We Bring Back Extinct Animals?" *National Geographic*, March 6, 2013. http://news.nationalgeographic.com /news/2013/03/130305-science-animals-extinct-species-revival-deextinction -debate-tedx/.

Sohn, Emily. "From Mammoth to Modern Elephant." *Science News for Students*, December 22, 2005. https://student.societyforscience.org/article/mammoth -modern-elephant.

"Southern Gastric-Brooding Frog (*Rheobactachus silus*)." Wildscreen Arkive. Accessed March 28, 2016. http://www.arkive.org/southern-gastric-brooding -frog/rheobatrachus-silus/.

Steadman, Ian. "Jurassic Park Impossible Because of Stupid Laws of Physics." *Wired UK*, October 10, 2012. http://www.wired.com/2012/10/jurassic-park -dna-half-life/.

Switek, Brian. "The Promise and Pitfalls of Resurrection Biology." *National Geographic*, March 12, 2013. http://phenomena.nationalgeographic.com /2013/03/12/the-promise-and-pitfalls-of-resurrection-ecology/.

"The Tasmanian Tiger." Australian Government. Accessed April 3, 2016. http:// www.australia.gov.au/about-australia/australian-story/tasmanian-tiger.

Watson, Julie. "Survival for Some Endangered Species Hinges on 'Frozen Zoo.'" *Washington Post*, February 17, 2015. https://www.washingtonpost.com /national/health-science/survival-for-some-endangered-species-hinges-on -frozen-zoo/2015/02/13/b79a579e-b201-11e4-827f-93f454140e2b_story.html.

"What Are the Risks of Cloning?" Learn.Genetics. Accessed April 9, 2016. http:// learn.genetics.utah.edu/content/cloning/cloningrisks/.

"Whooping Crane Comeback." Operation Migration. Accessed April 2, 2016. https://www.learner.org/jnorth/tm/crane/AboutFall.html.

Williams, Sarah C. P. "Humans Not Solely to Blame for Passenger Pigeon Extinction." *Science*, June 16, 2014. http://www.sciencemag.org/news/2014 /06/humans-not-solely-blame-passenger-pigeon-extinction.

Wilson, Alexander. *American Ornithologist, or the Natural History of the Birds of the United States*. Philadelphia: Bradford and Inskeep, 1808.

Wolf, Adam. "The Big Thaw." *Stanford Alumni*, September/October 2008. https:// alumni.stanford.edu/get/page/magazine/article/?article_id=31018.

"Woolly Mammoth Revival." Long New Foundation. Accessed January 1, 2016. http://longnow.org/revive/woolly-mammoth/.

Yong, Ed. "Resurrecting the Extinct Frog with a Womb for a Stomach." *National Geographic*, March 15, 2013. http://phenomena.nationalgeographic.com /2013/03/15/resurrecting-the-extinct-frog-with-a-stomach-for-a-womb/.

Zimmer, Carl. "Bringing Them Back to Life." *National Geographic*, April 2013. http://ngm.nationalgeographic.com/2013/04/125-species-revival/zimmer -text.

———. "Century after Extinction, Passenger Pigeons Remain Iconic—and Scientists Hope to Bring Them Back." *National Geographic*, August 30, 2014. http://news.nationalgeographic.com/news/2014/08/140831-passenger -pigeon-martha-deextinction-dna-animals-species/.

———. "Resurrecting a Forest." *National Geographic*, March 11, 2013. http:// phenomena.nationalgeographic.com/2013/03/11/resurrecting-a-forest/.

Zimov, Sergey A. "Pleistocene Park: Return of the Mammoth's Ecosystem." *Science* 308 (2005): 796–798.

FURTHER INFORMATION

Books

Agenbroad, Larry D. *Mammoths: Ice-Age Giants*. Minneapolis: Lerner Publications, 2002.

Andryszewski, Tricia. *Mass Extinction: Examining the Current Crisis*. Minneapolis: Twenty-First Century Books, 2008.

Church, George M., and Ed Regis. *Regenesis: How Synthetic Biology Will Reinvent Nature and Ourselves*. Philadelphia: Perseus, 2012.

Downer, Ann. *Wild Animal Neighbors: Sharing Our Urban World*. Minneapolis: Twenty-First Century Books, 2014.

Freinkel, Susan. *American Chestnut: The Life, Death, and Rebirth of a Perfect Tree*. Berkeley: University of California Press, 2009.

Fuller, Errol. *Lost Animals: Extinction and the Photographic Record*. Princeton, NJ: Princeton University Press, 2014.

Greenberg, Joel. *A Feathered River across the Sky: The Passenger Pigeon's Flight to Extinction*. New York: Bloomsbury, 2014.

Hoose, Phillip M. *The Race to Save the Lord God Bird*. New York: Farrar, Straus and Giroux, 2014.

Lister, Adrian, and Paul Bahn. *Mammoths: Giants of the Ice Age*. New York: Chartwell Books, 2015.

McPherson, Stephanie Sammartino. *Arctic Thaw: Climate Change and the Global Race for Energy Resources*. Minneapolis: Twenty-First Century Books, 2015.

Mukherjee, Siddhartha. *The Gene: An Intimate History*. New York: Scribner, 2016.

Sartore, Joel. *Rare: Portraits of America's Endangered Species*. Washington, DC: Focal Point, 2010.

Shapiro, Beth. *How to Clone a Mammoth: The Science of De-extinction*. Princeton, NJ: Princeton University Press, 2015.

Video

The Collectors: The Case for De-extinction. Bristol, CT: FiveThirtyEight, ESPN Films, 2015.
http://espn.go.com/video/clip?id=14765186
This short documentary film follows Australian paleontologist Michael Archer as he collects bones, DNA, and vital data from the extinct Tasmanian tiger and talks about the possibility of bringing animals back from extinction.

Websites

The American Chestnut Foundation
> http://www.acf.org
> The effort to revive the American chestnut tree is about forty years ahead
> of all other de-extinction efforts, having started around 1980. Learn
> more about the work being done to restore this iconic tree to the eastern
> woodlands.

Center for Biological Diversity
> http://www.biologicaldiversity.org
> Biological diversity is critical to the health of ecosystems, because
> plants and animals—including humans—depend on one another for
> survival. The Center for Biological Diversity promotes legal, scientific, and
> educational efforts to protect the diversity of species on Earth.

Frozen Zoo
> http://institute.sandiegozoo.org/resources/frozen-zoo®
> Part of the San Diego Zoo's Institute for Conservation Research, the Frozen
> Zoo holds more than ten thousand cell cultures and embryos of nearly one
> thousand different kinds of animals. The zoo's website describes efforts to
> breed endangered species using reproductive technology such as in vitro
> fertilization and artificial insemination.

IUCN Red List of Threatened Species.
> http://www.iucnredlist.org/
> The Red List, maintained by the International Union for Conservation
> of Nature, is the world's most comprehensive listing of endangered and
> threatened species. On the Red List website, you can search for a species
> and get detailed information about its biology, current habitat, threats, and
> endangered status.

Learn.Genetics: Cloning
> http://learn.genetics.utah.edu/content/cloning/
> This website from the Genetic Science Learning Center at the University
> of Utah provides an introduction to the science and history of cloning.
> You can even try your hand at cloning a mouse using the site's "Click and
> Clone" feature.

Long Now Foundation: Revive & Restore
> http://longnow.org/revive/
> Revive & Restore is dedicated to the genetic rescue of endangered and
> extinct species. The group's website offers information about projects to
> bring back the woolly mammoth and the passenger pigeon.

The Long Now Foundation: TEDxDeExtinction
> http://tedxdeextinction.org
> At this website, you can watch all the talks from the TEDxDeExtinction
> meeting held at National Geographic headquarters in 2013.

National Geographic: De-extinction

http://www.nationalgeographic.com/deextinction

National Geographic's de-extinction hub features news, articles, and debates about whether we should try to resurrect extinct species.

The Photo Ark

http://www.joelsartore.com/galleries/the-photo-ark/

The website of *National Geographic* photographer Joel Sartore includes photos of endangered animals from zoos and aquariums. Sartore's mission is to photograph as many endangered animals as he can before they go extinct. Several animals in the Photo Ark have gone extinct since Sartore took their pictures.

The Sixth Extinction

http://www.petermaas.nl/extinct/index.html

This website has a wealth of information on the extinction crisis, recently extinct plants and animals, and personal actions you can take to protect biodiversity.

INDEX

PHOTO ACKNOWLEDGMENTS

The images in this book are used with the permission of: Biodiversity Heritage Library, p. 4; © Getty Images, p. 7; © Laura Westlund/Independent Picture Service, pp. 8, 11, 13, 15; © Photoshot License Ltd/Alamy, p. 16; © Mark Carwardine/Photolibrary/Getty Images, p. 19; © Janette Hill/Alamy, p. 21; © 2008 Public Library of Science/Wikimedia Commons (CC BY 2.5), p. 24; ITAR-TASS/Andrei Tkachev/Newscom, p. 26; © Laura Westlund/Independent Picture Service, p. 28; © Science Source/Getty Images, p. 32; Brian Harris/REX/Shutterstock, p. 34; © Luis Davilla/PhotoLibrary/Getty Images, p. 36; Sergey Gorshkov/ Minden Pictures/Newscom, p. 38; © AB Apana/Moment/Getty Images, p. 42; AP Photo/Lisa Poole, p. 43; © Laura Westlund/Independent Picture Service, p. 45; © Hannes Grobe, AWI/Wikimedia Commons (CC-BY-SA-2.5), p. 48; © Gordon Wiltsie/National Geographic/Getty Images, p. 53; © Smith Bennett/Wikimedia Commons (public domain), p. 54; © liszt collection/Alamy, p. 59; © Bristol City Museum/npl/Minden Pictures, p. 61; Geoff Swaine/Photoshot//Newscom, p. 62; The Granger Collection, New York, p. 66; © GAP Photos/FhF Greenmedia, p. 67; Tom Lynn/Milwaukee Journal Sentinel/TNS/Newscom, p. 72; © Michael J. Tyler/Science Source, p. 74; © Nature Source/Science Source, p. 80 (right); © Krystyna Szulecka Photography/Alamy, p. 80 (left); © Roger de la Harpe/SuperStock, p. 84; © Horizons WWP/TRVL/Alamy, p. 86; Charlie Neuman/UT San Diego/Copyright 2014 San Diego Union-Tribune, LLC/Newscom, p. 88; AP Photo/Lenny Ignelz, p. 91; © John E Marriott/All Canada Photos/Getty Images, p. 92; © Josef Vostarek/CTK/Alamy, p. 94; Brianna Soukup/ZUMA Press/Newscom, p. 96.

Front cover: © iStockphoto.com/Aunt_Spray; back cover: © iStockphoto.com/wavemovies (dirt background).

ABOUT THE AUTHOR

Rebecca E. Hirsch has written about science and discovery in dozens of books for children and young adults. One of her newest titles is *The Human Microbiome: The Germs That Keep You Healthy*, a Junior Library Guild selection. A former scientist, she holds a PhD in cellular and molecular biology from the University of Wisconsin. She lives in State College, Pennsylvania, with her husband, Rick; their three daughters; and various pets. You can learn more at her website: www.rebeccahirsch.com.